Just The
factsl0l
Textbook Key Facts

Textbook Outlines, Highlights, and Practice Quizzes

Cost Accounting

by Charles T. Horngren, 15th Edition

All "Just the Facts101" Material Written or Prepared by Cram101 Textbook Reviews

Title Page

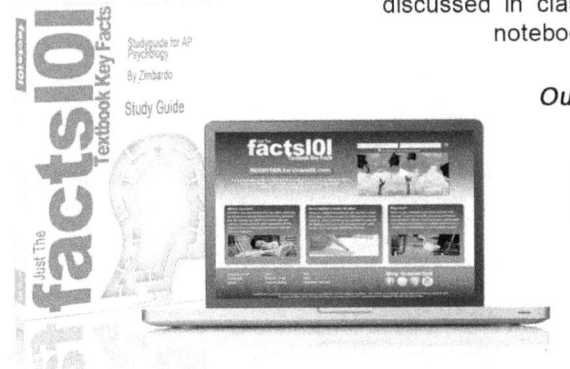

facts101
LEARNING SYSTEM

"Just the Facts101" is a Content Technologies publication and tool designed to give you all the facts from your textbooks. Visit JustTheFacts101.com for the full practice test for each of your chapters for virtually any of your textbooks.

Facts101 has built custom study tools specific to your textbook. We provide all of the factual testable information and unlike traditional study guides, we will never send you back to your textbook for more information.

YOU WILL NEVER HAVE TO HIGHLIGHT A BOOK AGAIN!

Facts101 StudyGuides

All of the information in this StudyGuide is written specifically for your textbook. We include the key terms, places, people, and concepts... the information you can expect on your next exam!

Want to take a practice test?

Throughout each chapter of this StudyGuide you will find links to JustTheFacts101.com where you can select specific chapters to take a complete test on, or you can subscribe and get practice tests for up to 12 of your textbooks, along with other exclusive Jtf101.com tools like problem solving labs and reference libraries.

JustTheFacts101.com

Only Jtf101.com gives you the outlines, highlights, and PRACTICE TESTS specific to your textbook. JustTheFacts101.com is an online application where you'll discover study tools designed to make the most of your limited study time.

By purchasing this book, you get 50% off the normal monthly subscription fee!. Just enter the promotional code **'DK73DW24914'** on the Jtf101.com registration screen.

www.JustTheFacts101.com

ISBN(s): 9781497007208. PUBX-6.201456

Cost Accounting
Charles T. Horngren, 15th

CONTENTS

1. The Manager and Management Accounting

CHAPTER OUTLINE: KEY TERMS, PEOPLE, PLACES, CONCEPTS

Enterprise resource planning

Management accounting

Accounting management

Process costing

Customer relationship management

Supply chain

Perfectly competitive

Sustainability

Total Quality Management

Belief systems

Decision-making process

Management control

Cost reduction

Chief financial officer

Investor relations

Line management

Risk management

Strategic planning

Error term

Professional ethics

1. The Manager and Management Accounting

Enterprise resource planning	Enterprise resource planning is a business management software--usually a suite of integrated applications--that a company can use to store and manage data from every stage of business, including:
	Enterprise resource planning provides an integrated real-time view of core business processes, using common databases maintained by a database management system. Enterprise resource planning systems track business resources--cash, raw materials, production capacity--and the status of business commitments: orders, purchase orders, and payroll. The applications that make up the system share data across the various departments (manufacturing, purchasing, sales, accounting, etc).
Management accounting	Management accounting or managerial accounting is concerned with the provisions and use of accounting information to managers within organizations, to provide them with the basis to make informed business decisions that will allow them to be better equipped in their management and control functions.
	In contrast to financial accountancy information, management accounting information is:•primarily forward-looking, instead of historical•model based with a degree of abstraction to support decision making generically, instead of case based;•designed and intended for use by managers within the organization, instead of being intended for use by shareholders, creditors, and public regulators;•usually confidential and used by management, instead of publicly reported;•computed by reference to the needs of managers, often using management information systems, instead of by reference to general financial accounting standards.
Accounting management	Accounting Management is the practical application of management techniques to control and report on the financial health of the organization. This involves the analysis, planning, implementation, and control of programs designed to provide financial data reporting for managerial decision making. This includes the maintenance of bank accounts, developing financial statements, cash flow and financial performance analysis.
Process costing	Process costing is a accounting methodology that traces and accumulates direct costs, and allocates indirect costs of a manufacturing process. Costs are assigned to products, usually in a large batch, which might include an entire month's production. Eventually, costs have to be allocated to individual units of product.
Customer relationship management	Customer relationship management Is a system for managing a company's interactions with current and future customers. It involves using technology to organize, automate and synchronize sales, marketing, customer service, and technical support.
Supply chain	A supply chain is a system of organizations, people, activities, information, and resources involved in moving a product or service from supplier to customer.

	Supply chain activities transform natural resources, raw materials, and components into a finished product that is delivered to the end customer. In sophisticated supply chain systems, used products may re-enter the supply chain at any point where residual value is recyclable.
Perfectly competitive	In economic theory, perfect competition describes markets such that no participants are large enough to have the market power to set the price of a homogeneous product. Because the conditions for perfect competition are strict, there are few if any perfectly competitive markets. Still, buyers and sellers in some auction-type markets, say for commodities or some financial assets, may approximate the concept.
Sustainability	In ecology, sustainability is how biological systems endure and remain diverse and productive. Long-lived and healthy wetlands and forests are examples of sustainable biological systems. In more general terms, sustainability refers to the endurance of systems and processes.
Total Quality Management	Total quality management consists of organization-wide efforts to install and make permanent a climate in which an organization continuously improves its ability to deliver high-quality products and services to customers. While there is no widely agreed-upon approach, Total Quality Management efforts typically draw heavily on the previously-developed tools and techniques of quality control. Total Quality Management enjoyed widespread attention during the late 1980s and early 1990s before being overshadowed by ISO 9000, Lean manufacturing, and Six Sigma.
Belief systems	A belief system is a set of mutually supportive beliefs. The beliefs of any such system can be classified as religious, philosophical, ideological, or a combination of these. Philosopher Jonathan Glover says that beliefs are always part of a belief system, and that belief systems are difficult to completely revise.
Decision-making process	Decision-making can be regarded as the cognitive process resulting in the selection of a belief or a course of action among several alternative possibilities. Every decision-making process produces a final choice that may or may not prompt action. Decision making is one of the central activities of management and is a huge part of any process of implementation.
Management control	A management control system is a system which gathers and uses information to evaluate the performance of different organizational resources like human, physical, financial and also the organization as a whole considering the organizational strategies. Finally, MCS influences the behavior of organizational resources to implement organizational strategies. MCS might be formal or informal.
Cost reduction	Cost reduction is the process used by companies to reduce their costs and increase their profits. Depending on a company's services or Product, the strategies can vary. Every decision in the product development process affects cost.
Chief financial officer	The chief financial officer or chief financial and operating officer (CFOO) is a corporate officer primarily responsible for managing the financial risks of the corporation.

1. The Manager and Management Accounting

	This officer is also responsible for financial planning and record-keeping, as well as financial reporting to higher management. In some sectors the Chief financial officer is also responsible for analysis of data.
Investor relations	Investor Relations is a strategic management responsibility that is capable of integrating finance, communication, marketing and securities law compliance to enable the most effective two-way communication between a company, the financial community, and other constituencies, which ultimately contributes to a company's securities achieving fair valuation. (Adopted by the NIRI Board of Directors, March 2003). The term describes the department of a company devoted to handling inquiries from shareholders and investors, as well as others who might be interested in a company's stock or financial stability.
Line management	Line Management is a business term to describe the administration of activities that contribute directly to the output of products or services. In corporate hierarchy, a Line Manager holds authority in a vertical (chain of command), and/or over a particular product line. He or she is charged with meeting corporate objectives in a specific functional area or line of business.
Risk management	Risk management is the identification, assessment, and prioritization of risks followed by coordinated and economical application of resources to minimize, monitor, and control the probability and/or impact of unfortunate events or to maximize the realization of opportunities. Risks can come from uncertainty in financial markets, threats from project failures (at any phase in design, development, production, or sustainment life-cycles), legal liabilities, credit risk, accidents, natural causes and disasters as well as deliberate attack from an adversary, or events of uncertain or unpredictable root-cause. Several risk management standards have been developed including the Project Management Institute, the National Institute of Standards and Technology, actuarial societies, and ISO standards.
Strategic planning	Strategic planning is an organization's process of defining its strategy, or direction, and making decisions on allocating its resources to pursue this strategy.
	In order to determine the future direction of the organization, it is necessary to understand its current position and the possible avenues through which it can pursue particular courses of action. Generally, strategic planning deals with at least one of three key questions:•'What do we do?'•'For whom do we do it?'•'How do we excel?'
	George Friedman in The Next 100 Years summarises 'the fundamental principle of strategic planning: hope for the best, plan for the worst'.
Error term	An error term is an additive type of error. Common examples include:•errors and residuals in statistics, e.g. in linear regression•the error term in numerical integration.

Professional ethics	Professional ethics encompass the personal, organizational and corporate standards of behaviour expected of professionals.
	Professionals, and those working in acknowledged professions, exercise specialist knowledge and skill. How the use of this knowledge should be governed when providing a service to the public can be considered a moral issue and is termed professional ethics.

CHAPTER QUIZ: KEY TERMS, PEOPLE, PLACES, CONCEPTS

1. _____ is a business management software--usually a suite of integrated applications--that a company can use to store and manage data from every stage of business, including:

   _____ provides an integrated real-time view of core business processes, using common databases maintained by a database management system. _____ systems track business resources--cash, raw materials, production capacity--and the status of business commitments: orders, purchase orders, and payroll. The applications that make up the system share data across the various departments (manufacturing, purchasing, sales, accounting, etc).

   a. Inter Revisjon
   b. Accountant
   c. Enterprise resource planning
   d. Indian Chartered Accountancy Course

2. _____ or managerial accounting is concerned with the provisions and use of accounting information to managers within organizations, to provide them with the basis to make informed business decisions that will allow them to be better equipped in their management and control functions.

   In contrast to financial accountancy information, _____ information is:•primarily forward-looking, instead of historical•model based with a degree of abstraction to support decision making generically, instead of case based;•designed and intended for use by managers within the organization, instead of being intended for use by shareholders, creditors, and public regulators;•usually confidential and used by management, instead of publicly reported;•computed by reference to the needs of managers, often using management information systems, instead of by reference to general financial accounting standards.

   a. Balance
   b. Management accounting
   c. Capital expenditure
   d. Cash flow

1. The Manager and Management Accounting

3. A _____(s) is a set of mutually supportive beliefs. The beliefs of any such system can be classified as religious, philosophical, ideological, or a combination of these. Philosopher Jonathan Glover says that beliefs are always part of a _____(s), and that _____ are difficult to completely revise.

   a. Belief systems
   b. Health Care and Education Reconciliation Act
   c. Social Security Act
   d. Constraints accounting

4. _____ is a system for managing a company's interactions with current and future customers. It involves using technology to organize, automate and synchronize sales, marketing, customer service, and technical support.

   a. Consumer Credit Protection Act
   b. Breakage
   c. Customer relationship management
   d. Constraints accounting

5. _____ is an organization's process of defining its strategy, or direction, and making decisions on allocating its resources to pursue this strategy.

   In order to determine the future direction of the organization, it is necessary to understand its current position and the possible avenues through which it can pursue particular courses of action. Generally, _____ deals with at least one of three key questions:•'What do we do?'•'For whom do we do it?'•'How do we excel?'

   George Friedman in The Next 100 Years summarises 'the fundamental principle of _____: hope for the best, plan for the worst'.

   a. supplier evaluation
   b. Strategic planning
   c. Health Care and Education Reconciliation Act
   d. Circulation Verification Council

1. c
2. b
3. a
4. c
5. b

You can take the complete Chapter Practice Test

for 1. The Manager and Management Accounting
on all key terms, persons, places, and concepts.

Online 99 Cents

http://www.JustTheFacts101.com

Use www.JustTheFacts101.com for all your study needs

including Facts101's online interactive problem solving labs in

chemistry, statistics, mathematics, and more.

2. An Introduction to Cost Terms and Purposes

CHAPTER OUTLINE: KEY TERMS, PEOPLE, PLACES, CONCEPTS

_____ | Cost object

_____ | Cost reduction

_____ | Cost allocation

_____ | Assignment

_____ | Indirect costs

_____ | Job costing

_____ | Fixed cost

_____ | Total cost

_____ | Variable cost

_____ | Cost driver

_____ | Activity-based costing

_____ | Average Cost

_____ | Unit cost

_____ | Finished good

_____ | Manufacturing cost

_____ | Factory overhead

_____ | Manufacturing overhead

_____ | Operating income

_____ | Overtime

2. An Introduction to Cost Terms and Purposes

Cost object	A cost object is a tangible input for a product manufactured/service provided, like labor or material. For example a cloth manufacturing firm requires some amount of predetermined labor and predetermined raw material for any amount of cloth being manufactured. The cost of employing labor can be directly fixed as 'per man per hour' or 'per man per day per hour per minute per annum', so the labor is a cost object as you can directly associate cost with it.
Cost reduction	Cost reduction is the process used by companies to reduce their costs and increase their profits. Depending on a company's services or Product, the strategies can vary. Every decision in the product development process affects cost.
Cost allocation	Cost allocation is a process of providing relief to shared service organization's cost centers that provide a product or service. In turn, the associated expense is assigned to internal clients' cost centers that consume the products and services. For example, the CIO may provide all IT services within the company and assign the costs back to the business units that consume each offering.
Assignment	An assignment is a term used with similar meanings in the law of contracts and in the law of real estate. In both instances, it encompasses the transfer of rights held by one party--the assignor--to another party--the assignee. The details of the assignment determines some additional rights and liabilities (or duties).
Indirect costs	Indirect costs are costs that are not directly accountable to a cost object . Indirect costs may be either fixed or variable. Indirect costs include administration, personnel and security costs.
Job costing	Job Costing involves the calculation of costs involved in a construction 'job' or the manufacturing of goods done in discrete batches. These costs are recorded in ledger accounts throughout the life of the job or batch and are then summarized in the final trial balance before the preparing of the job cost or batch manufacturing statement.
Fixed cost	In economics, fixed costs, indirect costs or overheads are business expenses that are not dependent on the level of goods or services produced by the business. They tend to be time-related, such as salaries or rents being paid per month, and are often referred to as overhead costs. This is in contrast to variable costs, which are volume-related (and are paid per quantity produced).
Total cost	In economics, and cost accounting, total cost describes the total economic cost of production and is made up of variable costs, which vary according to the quantity of a good produced and include inputs such as labor and raw materials, plus fixed costs, which are independent of the quantity of a good produced and include inputs (capital) that cannot be varied in the short term, such as buildings and machinery. Total cost in economics includes the total opportunity cost of each factor of production as part of its fixed or variable costs. The rate at which total cost changes as the amount produced changes is called marginal cost.

2. An Introduction to Cost Terms and Purposes

Variable cost	Variable costs are costs that change in proportion to the good or service that a business produces. Variable costs are also the sum of marginal costs over all units produced. They can also be considered normal costs.
Cost driver	According to CIMA, 'cost driver is any factor which causes a change in the cost of an activity. A cost driver is the unit of an activity that causes the change in activity's cost. Examples: In marketing, cost drivers are Number of advertisements, Number of sales personnel etc.
Activity-based costing	Activity-based costing is a costing methodology that identifies activities in an organization and assigns the cost of each activity with resources to all products and services according to the actual consumption by each. This model assigns more indirect costs (overhead) into direct costs compared to conventional costing. CIMA (Chartered Institute of Management Accountants) defines Activity based costing as an approach to the costing and monitoring of activities which involves tracing resource consumption and costing final outputs.
Average Cost	Under the 'Average Cost Method', it is assumed that the cost of inventory is based on the average cost of the goods available for sale during the period. The average cost is computed by dividing the total cost of goods available for sale by the total units available for sale. This gives a weighted-average unit cost that is applied to the units in the ending inventory.
Unit cost	The unit cost is the cost incurred by a company to produce, store and sell one unit of a particular product. Unit costs include all fixed costs and all variable costs involved in production.
Finished good	Finished goods are goods that have completed the manufacturing process but have not yet been sold or distributed to the end user.
Manufacturing cost	Manufacturing cost is the sum of costs of all resources consumed in the process of making a product. The manufacturing cost is classified into three categories: direct materials cost, direct labor cost and manufacturing overhead.
Factory overhead	Factory overhead, also called manufacturing overhead or factory burden, is the total cost involved in operating all production facilities of a manufacturing business. It generally applies to indirect labor and indirect cost, it also includes all costs involved in manufacturing with the exception of the cost of raw materials and direct labor. Factory overhead also includes certain costs such as quality assurance costs, cleanup costs, and property insurance premiums.
Manufacturing overhead	Manufacturing overhead costs are all manufacturing costs that are related to the cost object (work in process and then finished goods) but cannot be traced to that cost object in an economically feasible way.

2. An Introduction to Cost Terms and Purposes

Examples include supplies, indirect materials such as lubricants, indirect manufacturing labor such as plant maintenance and cleaning labor, plant rent, plant insurance, property taxes on the plant, plant depreciation, and the compensation of plant managers.

This cost category is also referred to as Factory overhead cost (FO cost).

Operating income

In accounting and finance, earnings before interest and taxes, is a measure of a firm's profit that excludes interest and income tax expenses. It is the difference between operating revenues and operating expenses. When a firm does not have non-operating income, then operating income is sometimes used as a synonym for EBIT and operating profit.

Overtime

Overtime is the amount of time someone works beyond normal working hours. Normal hours may be determined in several ways:•by custom (what is considered healthy or reasonable by society),•by practices of a given trade or profession,•by legislation,•by agreement between employers and workers or their representatives.

Most nations have overtime labor laws designed to dissuade or prevent employers from forcing their employees to work excessively long hours. These laws may take into account other considerations than the humanitarian, such as preserving the health of workers so that they may continue to be productive, or increasing the overall level of employment in the economy.

1. _____s are goods that have completed the manufacturing process but have not yet been sold or distributed to the end user.

   a. Finished good
   b. Cost of goods available for sale
   c. Cost of goods sold
   d. Decomposition

2. . A _____ is a tangible input for a product manufactured/service provided, like labor or material. For example a cloth manufacturing firm requires some amount of predetermined labor and predetermined raw material for any amount of cloth being manufactured. The cost of employing labor can be directly fixed as 'per man per hour' or 'per man per day per hour per minute per annum', so the labor is a _____ as you can directly associate cost with it.

   a. Consumer Credit Protection Act

    b. Cost object

    c. Social Security Act

    d. Bachelor tax

3. _____ is the amount of time someone works beyond normal working hours. Normal hours may be determined in several ways:•by custom (what is considered healthy or reasonable by society),•by practices of a given trade or profession,•by legislation,•by agreement between employers and workers or their representatives.

Most nations have _____ labor laws designed to dissuade or prevent employers from forcing their employees to work excessively long hours. These laws may take into account other considerations than the humanitarian, such as preserving the health of workers so that they may continue to be productive, or increasing the overall level of employment in the economy.

    a. Inter Revisjon

    b. Breakage

    c. Overtime

    d. Constraints accounting

4. _____, also called manufacturing overhead or factory burden, is the total cost involved in operating all production facilities of a manufacturing business. It generally applies to indirect labor and indirect cost, it also includes all costs involved in manufacturing with the exception of the cost of raw materials and direct labor. _____ also includes certain costs such as quality assurance costs, cleanup costs, and property insurance premiums.

    a. Backflush accounting

    b. Breakage

    c. Break-even

    d. Factory overhead

5. _____ is a process of providing relief to shared service organization's cost centers that provide a product or service. In turn, the associated expense is assigned to internal clients' cost centers that consume the products and services. For example, the CIO may provide all IT services within the company and assign the costs back to the business units that consume each offering.

    a. Bank examiner

    b. Bookkeeping

    c. Cost allocation

    d. Carbon accounting

1. a
2. b
3. c
4. d
5. c

3. Cost—Volume—Profit Analysis

CHAPTER OUTLINE: KEY TERMS, PEOPLE, PLACES, CONCEPTS

	CVP analysis
	Contribution margin
	Decision-making process
	Total cost
	Quality management
	Operating income
	Cost reduction
	Fixed cost
	Net income
	Variable cost
	Sensitivity analysis
	Cost driver
	Operating leverage
	Leverage
	Gross margin
	Probability distribution
	Decision table

3. Cost—Volume—Profit Analysis

CVP analysis	Cost-volume-profit, in managerial economics, is a form of cost accounting. It is a simplified model, useful for elementary instruction and for short-run decisions.
	CVP analysis expands the use of information provided by breakeven analysis.
Contribution margin	Contribution margin is the dollar contribution per unit divided by the selling price per unit. "Contribution" represents the portion of sales revenue that is not consumed by variable costs and so contributes to the coverage of fixed costs. This concept is one of the key building blocks of break-even analysis.
Decision-making process	Decision-making can be regarded as the cognitive process resulting in the selection of a belief or a course of action among several alternative possibilities. Every decision-making process produces a final choice that may or may not prompt action. Decision making is one of the central activities of management and is a huge part of any process of implementation.
Total cost	In economics, and cost accounting, total cost describes the total economic cost of production and is made up of variable costs, which vary according to the quantity of a good produced and include inputs such as labor and raw materials, plus fixed costs, which are independent of the quantity of a good produced and include inputs (capital) that cannot be varied in the short term, such as buildings and machinery. Total cost in economics includes the total opportunity cost of each factor of production as part of its fixed or variable costs.
	The rate at which total cost changes as the amount produced changes is called marginal cost.
Quality management	The term quality management has a specific meaning within many business sectors. This specific definition, which does not aim to assure 'good quality' by the more general definition, but rather to ensure that an organization or product is consistent, can be considered to have four main components: quality planning, quality control, quality assurance and quality improvement. Quality management is focused not only on product/service quality, but also the means to achieve it.
Operating income	In accounting and finance, earnings before interest and taxes, is a measure of a firm's profit that excludes interest and income tax expenses. It is the difference between operating revenues and operating expenses. When a firm does not have non-operating income, then operating income is sometimes used as a synonym for EBIT and operating profit.
Cost reduction	Cost reduction is the process used by companies to reduce their costs and increase their profits. Depending on a company's services or Product, the strategies can vary. Every decision in the product development process affects cost.
Fixed cost	In economics, fixed costs, indirect costs or overheads are business expenses that are not dependent on the level of goods or services produced by the business.

3. Cost—Volume—Profit Analysis

	They tend to be time-related, such as salaries or rents being paid per month, and are often referred to as overhead costs. This is in contrast to variable costs, which are volume-related (and are paid per quantity produced).
Net income	In business, net income - also referred to as the bottom line, net profit, or net earnings - is an entity's income minus cost of goods sold, expenses and taxes for an accounting period. It is computed as the residual of all revenues and gains over all expenses and losses for the period, and has also been defined as the net increase in stockholder's equity that results from a company's operations. In the context of the presentation of financial statements, the IFRS Foundation defines net income as synonymous with profit and loss.
Variable cost	Variable costs are costs that change in proportion to the good or service that a business produces. Variable costs are also the sum of marginal costs over all units produced. They can also be considered normal costs.
Sensitivity analysis	Sensitivity analysis is the study of how the uncertainty in the output of a mathematical model or system can be apportioned to different sources of uncertainty in its inputs. A related practice is uncertainty analysis, which has a greater focus on uncertainty quantification and propagation of uncertainty. Ideally, uncertainty and sensitivity analysis should be run in tandem.
Cost driver	According to CIMA, 'cost driver is any factor which causes a change in the cost of an activity. A cost driver is the unit of an activity that causes the change in activity's cost. Examples: In marketing, cost drivers are Number of advertisements, Number of sales personnel etc.
Operating leverage	Operating leverage is a measure of how revenue growth translates into growth in operating income. Leverage, and of how risky (volatile) a company's operating income is.
Leverage	In finance, leverage is a general term for any technique to multiply gains and losses. Most often this involves buying more of an asset by using borrowed funds. The belief is that the income from the asset will more than pay for the cost of borrowing.
Gross margin	Gross margin is the difference between revenue and cost before accounting for certain other costs. Generally, it is calculated as the selling price of an item, less the cost of goods sold (production or acquisition costs, essentially).
Probability distribution	In probability and statistics, a probability distribution assigns a probability to each measurable subset of the possible outcomes of a random experiment, survey, or procedure of statistical inference. Examples are found in experiments whose sample space is non-numerical, where the distribution would be a categorical distribution; experiments whose sample space is encoded by discrete random variables, where the distribution can be specified by a probability mass function; and experiments with sample spaces encoded by continuous random variables, where the distribution can be specified by a probability density function.

3. Cost—Volume—Profit Analysis

Decision table	Decision tables are a precise yet compact way to model complicated logic.
	Decision tables, like flowcharts and if-then-else and switch-case statements, associate conditions with actions to perform, but in many cases do so in a more elegant way.
	In the 1960s and 1970s a range of 'decision table based' languages such as Filetab were popular for business programming.

1. _____ is the dollar contribution per unit divided by the selling price per unit. "Contribution" represents the portion of sales revenue that is not consumed by variable costs and so contributes to the coverage of fixed costs. This concept is one of the key building blocks of break-even analysis.

   a. Backflush accounting
   b. Breakage
   c. Break-even
   d. Contribution margin

2. According to CIMA, '_____ is any factor which causes a change in the cost of an activity. A _____ is the unit of an activity that causes the change in activity's cost. Examples: In marketing, _____s are Number of advertisements, Number of sales personnel etc.

   a. Cost driver
   b. Breakage
   c. Break-even
   d. Constraints accounting

3. Cost-volume-profit, in managerial economics, is a form of cost accounting. It is a simplified model, useful for elementary instruction and for short-run decisions.

   _____ expands the use of information provided by breakeven analysis.

   a. Consumer Credit Protection Act
   b. Health Care and Education Reconciliation Act
   c. Social Security Act
   d. CVP analysis

3. Cost—Volume—Profit Analysis

4. _____ is the process used by companies to reduce their costs and increase their profits. Depending on a company's services or Product, the strategies can vary. Every decision in the product development process affects cost.

    a. Total cost
    b. manufacturing cost
    c. Consumer Credit Protection Act
    d. Cost reduction

5. In economics, and cost accounting, _____ describes the total economic cost of production and is made up of variable costs, which vary according to the quantity of a good produced and include inputs such as labor and raw materials, plus fixed costs, which are independent of the quantity of a good produced and include inputs (capital) that cannot be varied in the short term, such as buildings and machinery. _____ in economics includes the total opportunity cost of each factor of production as part of its fixed or variable costs.

    The rate at which _____ changes as the amount produced changes is called marginal cost.

    a. manufacturing cost
    b. Total cost
    c. Health Care and Education Reconciliation Act
    d. Constraints accounting

1. d
2. a
3. d
4. d
5. b

You can take the complete Chapter Practice Test

for 3. Cost—Volume—Profit Analysis
on all key terms, persons, places, and concepts.

Online 99 Cents

http://www.JustTheFacts101.com

Use www.JustTheFacts101.com for all your study needs

including Facts101's online interactive problem solving labs in

chemistry, statistics, mathematics, and more.

4. Job Costing

CHAPTER OUTLINE: KEY TERMS, PEOPLE, PLACES, CONCEPTS

Job costing

Cost allocation

Cost object

Cost reduction

Assignment

Indirect costs

Cost pool

Cost-plus contract

Process costing

Decision-making process

General ledger

Ledger

Manufacturing overhead

Subsidiary

Finished good

Ending inventory

4. Job Costing

Job costing	Job Costing involves the calculation of costs involved in a construction 'job' or the manufacturing of goods done in discrete batches. These costs are recorded in ledger accounts throughout the life of the job or batch and are then summarized in the final trial balance before the preparing of the job cost or batch manufacturing statement.
Cost allocation	Cost allocation is a process of providing relief to shared service organization's cost centers that provide a product or service. In turn, the associated expense is assigned to internal clients' cost centers that consume the products and services. For example, the CIO may provide all IT services within the company and assign the costs back to the business units that consume each offering.
Cost object	A cost object is a tangible input for a product manufactured/service provided, like labor or material. For example a cloth manufacturing firm requires some amount of predetermined labor and predetermined raw material for any amount of cloth being manufactured. The cost of employing labor can be directly fixed as 'per man per hour' or 'per man per day per hour per minute per annum', so the labor is a cost object as you can directly associate cost with it.
Cost reduction	Cost reduction is the process used by companies to reduce their costs and increase their profits. Depending on a company's services or Product, the strategies can vary. Every decision in the product development process affects cost.
Assignment	An assignment is a term used with similar meanings in the law of contracts and in the law of real estate. In both instances, it encompasses the transfer of rights held by one party--the assignor--to another party--the assignee. The details of the assignment determines some additional rights and liabilities (or duties).
Indirect costs	Indirect costs are costs that are not directly accountable to a cost object . Indirect costs may be either fixed or variable. Indirect costs include administration, personnel and security costs.
Cost pool	Cost pools is an accounting term that refers to groups of accounts serving to express the cost of goods and service allocable within a business or manufacturing organization. The principle behind the pool is to correlate direct and indirect costs with a specified cost driver, so to find out the total sum of expenses related to the manufacture of a product. While the exact construction cost pools differs, most companies choose to form numerical based sequences that can then be allocated to the desired project.
Cost-plus contract	A cost-plus contract, also termed a cost reimbursement contract, is a contract where a contractor is paid for all of its allowed expenses to a set limit plus additional payment to allow for a profit. Cost-reimbursement contracts contrast with fixed-price contract, in which the contractor is paid a negotiated amount regardless of incurred expenses. Cost-plus contracts first came into use in the United States during the World Wars to encourage wartime production by large American companies.

Process costing	Process costing is a accounting methodology that traces and accumulates direct costs, and allocates indirect costs of a manufacturing process. Costs are assigned to products, usually in a large batch, which might include an entire month's production. Eventually, costs have to be allocated to individual units of product.
Decision-making process	Decision-making can be regarded as the cognitive process resulting in the selection of a belief or a course of action among several alternative possibilities. Every decision-making process produces a final choice that may or may not prompt action. Decision making is one of the central activities of management and is a huge part of any process of implementation.
General ledger	A general ledger contains user-defined account codes and related dimensional codes for recording transformed different types of vouchers including on-balance-sheet, off-balance-sheet, post-balance sheet, financial and non-financial natures. In modern accounting software or ERP, the general ledger works as a central repository for accounting data transferred from all subledgers or modules like accounts payable, accounts receivable, cash management, fixed assets, purchasing and projects. The general ledger is the backbone of any accounting system which holds financial and non-financial data for an organization.
Ledger	Ledger is a command-line based double-entry accounting app. Accounting data is stored in a plain text file, using a simple format, which the users prepare themselves using other tools. Ledger does not write or modify data, it only parses the input data and produces reports.
Manufacturing overhead	Manufacturing overhead costs are all manufacturing costs that are related to the cost object (work in process and then finished goods) but cannot be traced to that cost object in an economically feasible way. Examples include supplies, indirect materials such as lubricants, indirect manufacturing labor such as plant maintenance and cleaning labor, plant rent, plant insurance, property taxes on the plant, plant depreciation, and the compensation of plant managers. This cost category is also referred to as Factory overhead cost (FO cost).
Subsidiary	A subsidiary, subsidiary company, daughter company, or sister company is a company that is completely or partly owned by another corporation that owns more than half of the subsidiary's stock, and which normally acts as a holding corporation which at least partly or a parent corporation, wholly controls the activities and policies of the daughter corporation. The subsidiary can be a company, corporation, or limited liability company. In some cases it is a government or state-owned enterprise.

4. Job Costing

Ending inventory	Ending inventory is the amount of inventory a company has in stock at the end of its fiscal year. It is closely related with ending inventory cost, which is the amount of money spent to get these goods in stock. It should be calculated at the lower of cost or market.

1. An _____ is a term used with similar meanings in the law of contracts and in the law of real estate. In both instances, it encompasses the transfer of rights held by one party--the assignor--to another party--the assignee. The details of the _____ determines some additional rights and liabilities (or duties).

   a. market capitalization
   b. Consumer Credit Protection Act
   c. Health Care and Education Reconciliation Act
   d. Assignment

2. _____ involves the calculation of costs involved in a construction 'job' or the manufacturing of goods done in discrete batches. These costs are recorded in ledger accounts throughout the life of the job or batch and are then summarized in the final trial balance before the preparing of the job cost or batch manufacturing statement.

   a. Job costing
   b. Breakage
   c. Break-even
   d. Constraints accounting

3. _____ costs are all manufacturing costs that are related to the cost object (work in process and then finished goods) but cannot be traced to that cost object in an economically feasible way.

   Examples include supplies, indirect materials such as lubricants, indirect manufacturing labor such as plant maintenance and cleaning labor, plant rent, plant insurance, property taxes on the plant, plant depreciation, and the compensation of plant managers.

   This cost category is also referred to as Factory overhead cost (FO cost).

   a. Consumer Credit Protection Act
   b. Manufacturing overhead
   c. Grisbi
   d. HomeBank

4. . _____ is a process of providing relief to shared service organization's cost centers that provide a product or service.

In turn, the associated expense is assigned to internal clients' cost centers that consume the products and services. For example, the CIO may provide all IT services within the company and assign the costs back to the business units that consume each offering.

a. Bank examiner
b. Bookkeeping
c. Business mileage reimbursement rate
d. Cost allocation

5. _____ are costs that are not directly accountable to a cost object . _____ may be either fixed or variable. _____ include administration, personnel and security costs.

a. Backflush accounting
b. Breakage
c. Indirect costs
d. Constraints accounting

1. d
2. a
3. b
4. d
5. c

You can take the complete Chapter Practice Test

for 4. Job Costing
on all key terms, persons, places, and concepts.

Online 99 Cents

http://www.JustTheFacts101.com

Use **www.JustTheFacts101.com** for all your study needs

including Facts101's online interactive problem solving labs in

chemistry, statistics, mathematics, and more.

5. Activity-Based Costing and Activity-Based Management

CHAPTER OUTLINE: KEY TERMS, PEOPLE, PLACES, CONCEPTS

	Activity-based costing
	Decision-making process
	Flexible manufacturing systems
	Job costing
	Cost reduction
	Activity-based management
	Process improvement
	Management process
	Merchandising

CHAPTER HIGHLIGHTS & NOTES: KEY TERMS, PEOPLE, PLACES, CONCEPTS

Activity-based costing	Activity-based costing is a costing methodology that identifies activities in an organization and assigns the cost of each activity with resources to all products and services according to the actual consumption by each. This model assigns more indirect costs (overhead) into direct costs compared to conventional costing. CIMA (Chartered Institute of Management Accountants) defines Activity based costing as an approach to the costing and monitoring of activities which involves tracing resource consumption and costing final outputs.
Decision-making process	Decision-making can be regarded as the cognitive process resulting in the selection of a belief or a course of action among several alternative possibilities. Every decision-making process produces a final choice that may or may not prompt action. Decision making is one of the central activities of management and is a huge part of any process of implementation.
Flexible manufacturing systems	A flexible manufacturing system is a manufacturing system in which there is some amount of flexibility that allows the system to react in case of changes, whether predicted or unpredicted.

5. Activity-Based Costing and Activity-Based Management

	This flexibility is generally considered to fall into two categories, which both contain numerous subcategories.
	Flexible manufacturing systems will be formed with help of Mechatronics and Robotics Technologies.
Job costing	Job Costing involves the calculation of costs involved in a construction 'job' or the manufacturing of goods done in discrete batches. These costs are recorded in ledger accounts throughout the life of the job or batch and are then summarized in the final trial balance before the preparing of the job cost or batch manufacturing statement.
Cost reduction	Cost reduction is the process used by companies to reduce their costs and increase their profits. Depending on a company's services or Product, the strategies can vary. Every decision in the product development process affects cost.
Activity-based management	Activity-based management is a method of identifying and evaluating activities that a business performs using activity-based costing to carry out a value chain analysis or a re-engineering initiative to improve strategic and operational decisions in an organization. Activity-based costing establishes relationships between overhead costs and activities so that overhead costs can be more precisely allocated to products, services, or customer segments. Activity-based management focuses on managing activities to reduce costs and improve customer value.
Process improvement	Business process improvement is a systematic approach to help an organization optimize its underlying processes to achieve more efficient results. The methodology was first documented in H. James Harrington's 1991 book Business Process Improvement. It is the methodology that both Process Redesign and Business Process Reengineering are based upon.
Management process	Management process is a process of planning and controlling the organizing and leading execution of any type of activity, such as:
	The organization's senior management is responsible for carrying out its management process. However, this is not always the case for all management processes, for example, it is the responsibility of the project manager to carry out a project management process.
Merchandising	In the broadest sense, merchandising is any practice which contributes to the sale of products to a retail consumer. At a retail in store level, merchandising refers to the variety of products available for sale and the display of those products in such a way that it stimulates interest and entices customers to make a purchase.
	In retail commerce, visual display merchandising means merchandise sales using product design, selection, packaging, pricing, and display that stimulates consumers to spend more.

5. Activity-Based Costing and Activity-Based Management

1. _____ is the process used by companies to reduce their costs and increase their profits. Depending on a company's services or Product, the strategies can vary. Every decision in the product development process affects cost.

   a. Total cost
   b. manufacturing cost
   c. Consumer Credit Protection Act
   d. Cost reduction

2. _____ is a costing methodology that identifies activities in an organization and assigns the cost of each activity with resources to all products and services according to the actual consumption by each. This model assigns more indirect costs (overhead) into direct costs compared to conventional costing.

   CIMA (Chartered Institute of Management Accountants) defines Activity based costing as an approach to the costing and monitoring of activities which involves tracing resource consumption and costing final outputs.

   a. Managerial risk accounting
   b. Variable Costing
   c. Activity-based costing
   d. BDO International

3. _____ involves the calculation of costs involved in a construction 'job' or the manufacturing of goods done in discrete batches. These costs are recorded in ledger accounts throughout the life of the job or batch and are then summarized in the final trial balance before the preparing of the job cost or batch manufacturing statement.

   a. Backflush accounting
   b. Job costing
   c. Break-even
   d. Constraints accounting

4. Business _____ is a systematic approach to help an organization optimize its underlying processes to achieve more efficient results. The methodology was first documented in H. James Harrington's 1991 book Business _____. It is the methodology that both Process Redesign and Business Process Reengineering are based upon.

   a. Consumer Credit Protection Act
   b. Variable Costing
   c. Bachelor tax
   d. Process improvement

5. . In the broadest sense, _____ is any practice which contributes to the sale of products to a retail consumer. At a retail in-store level, _____ refers to the variety of products available for sale and the display of those products in such a way that it stimulates interest and entices customers to make a purchase.

5. Activity-Based Costing and Activity-Based Management

In retail commerce, visual display _____ means merchandise sales using product design, selection, packaging, pricing, and display that stimulates consumers to spend more.

a. Merchandising
b. Variable Costing
c. Bachelor tax
d. BDO International

1. d
2. c
3. b
4. d
5. a

You can take the complete Chapter Practice Test

for 5. Activity-Based Costing and Activity-Based Management
on all key terms, persons, places, and concepts.

Online 99 Cents

http://www.JustTheFacts101.com

Use www.JustTheFacts101.com for all your study needs

including Facts101's online interactive problem solving labs in

chemistry, statistics, mathematics, and more.

6. Master Budget and Responsibility Accounting

CHAPTER OUTLINE: KEY TERMS, PEOPLE, PLACES, CONCEPTS

	Perfectly competitive
	On-time performance
	Bill of materials
	Manufacturing overhead
	Ending inventory
	Manufacturing cost
	Cost of goods sold
	Enterprise resource planning
	Sensitivity analysis
	Vendor-managed inventory
	Investment center
	Profit center
	Responsibility center
	Revenue center
	Control charts
	Cost reduction
	Error term
	Cash flow

6. Master Budget and Responsibility Accounting

Perfectly competitive	In economic theory, perfect competition describes markets such that no participants are large enough to have the market power to set the price of a homogeneous product. Because the conditions for perfect competition are strict, there are few if any perfectly competitive markets. Still, buyers and sellers in some auction-type markets, say for commodities or some financial assets, may approximate the concept.
On-time performance	In transportation, such as municipal public transportation, schedule adherence or on-time performance refers to the level of success of the service remaining on the published schedule.
Bill of materials	A bill of materials is a list of the raw materials, sub-assemblies, intermediate assemblies, sub-components, parts and the quantities of each needed to manufacture an end product. A Bill of materials may be used for communication between manufacturing partners, or confined to a single manufacturing plant. A Bill of materials can define products as they are designed (engineering bill of materials), as they are ordered (sales bill of materials), as they are built (manufacturing bill of materials), or as they are maintained (service bill of materials).
Manufacturing overhead	Manufacturing overhead costs are all manufacturing costs that are related to the cost object (work in process and then finished goods) but cannot be traced to that cost object in an economically feasible way. Examples include supplies, indirect materials such as lubricants, indirect manufacturing labor such as plant maintenance and cleaning labor, plant rent, plant insurance, property taxes on the plant, plant depreciation, and the compensation of plant managers. This cost category is also referred to as Factory overhead cost (FO cost).
Ending inventory	Ending inventory is the amount of inventory a company has in stock at the end of its fiscal year. It is closely related with ending inventory cost, which is the amount of money spent to get these goods in stock. It should be calculated at the lower of cost or market.
Manufacturing cost	Manufacturing cost is the sum of costs of all resources consumed in the process of making a product. The manufacturing cost is classified into three categories: direct materials cost, direct labor cost and manufacturing overhead.
Cost of goods sold	Cost of goods sold refer to the carrying value of goods sold during a particular period. Costs are associated with particular goods using one of several formulas, including specific identification, first-in first-out, or average cost.

6. Master Budget and Responsibility Accounting

Enterprise resource planning	Enterprise resource planning is a business management software--usually a suite of integrated applications--that a company can use to store and manage data from every stage of business, including: Enterprise resource planning provides an integrated real-time view of core business processes, using common databases maintained by a database management system. Enterprise resource planning systems track business resources--cash, raw materials, production capacity--and the status of business commitments: orders, purchase orders, and payroll. The applications that make up the system share data across the various departments (manufacturing, purchasing, sales, accounting, etc).
Sensitivity analysis	Sensitivity analysis is the study of how the uncertainty in the output of a mathematical model or system can be apportioned to different sources of uncertainty in its inputs. A related practice is uncertainty analysis, which has a greater focus on uncertainty quantification and propagation of uncertainty. Ideally, uncertainty and sensitivity analysis should be run in tandem.
Vendor-managed inventory	Vendor-managed inventory is a family of business models in which the buyer of a product (business) provides certain information to a vendor (supply chain) supplier of that product and the supplier takes full responsibility for maintaining an agreed inventory of the material, usually at the buyer's consumption location (usually a store). A third-party logistics provider can also be involved to make sure that the buyer has the required level of inventory by adjusting the demand and supply gaps. As a symbiotic relationship, Vendor managed inventory makes it less likely that a business will unintentionally become out of stock of a good and reduces inventory in the supply chain.
Investment center	An investment center is a classification used for business units within an enterprise. The essential element of an investment center is that it is treated as a unit which is measured against its use of capital, as opposed to a cost or profit center, which are measured against raw costs or profits. The Investment Center takes care of Revenues, Cost and Assets -while Profit Center deal just with revenues and costs and Cost Center with cost only.
Profit center	A profit center is a part of a corporation that directly adds to its profit.
Responsibility center	A responsibility center is an organization unit that is headed by a manager who is responsible for its activities and results. In Responsibility Accounting revenues and costs information are collected and reported by responsibility centers.
Revenue center	In business, a revenue centre or revenue center is a division that gains revenue from product sales or service provided. The manager in revenue centre is accountable for revenue only.

6. Master Budget and Responsibility Accounting

Control charts	Control charts, also known as Shewhart charts or process-behavior charts, in statistical process control are tools used to determine if a manufacturing or business process is in a state of statistical control.
Cost reduction	Cost reduction is the process used by companies to reduce their costs and increase their profits. Depending on a company's services or Product, the strategies can vary. Every decision in the product development process affects cost.
Error term	An error term is an additive type of error. Common examples include:•errors and residuals in statistics, e.g. in linear regression•the error term in numerical integration.
Cash flow	Cash flow is the movement of money into or out of a business, project, or financial product. It is usually measured during a specified, limited period of time. Measurement of cash flow can be used for calculating other parameters that give information on a company's value and situation.

1. _____ is a family of business models in which the buyer of a product (business) provides certain information to a vendor (supply chain) supplier of that product and the supplier takes full responsibility for maintaining an agreed inventory of the material, usually at the buyer's consumption location (usually a store). A third-party logistics provider can also be involved to make sure that the buyer has the required level of inventory by adjusting the demand and supply gaps.

   As a symbiotic relationship, Vendor managed inventory makes it less likely that a business will unintentionally become out of stock of a good and reduces inventory in the supply chain.

   a. Vendor-managed inventory
   b. Consumer Credit Protection Act
   c. Health Care and Education Reconciliation Act
   d. Check register

2. . A _____ is a list of the raw materials, sub-assemblies, intermediate assemblies, sub-components, parts and the quantities of each needed to manufacture an end product. A _____ may be used for communication between manufacturing partners, or confined to a single manufacturing plant.

   A _____ can define products as they are designed (engineering _____), as they are ordered (sales _____), as they are built (manufacturing _____), or as they are maintained (service _____).

   a. Consumer Credit Protection Act
   b. Health Care and Education Reconciliation Act

c. Social Security Act

d. Bill of materials

3. In economic theory, perfect competition describes markets such that no participants are large enough to have the market power to set the price of a homogeneous product. Because the conditions for perfect competition are strict, there are few if any _____ markets. Still, buyers and sellers in some auction-type markets, say for commodities or some financial assets, may approximate the concept.

a. Perfectly competitive

b. Health Care and Education Reconciliation Act

c. Social Security Act

d. Bachelor tax

4. _____ is the amount of inventory a company has in stock at the end of its fiscal year. It is closely related with _____ cost, which is the amount of money spent to get these goods in stock. It should be calculated at the lower of cost or market.

a. Carrying cost

b. Ending inventory

c. Cost of goods sold

d. Decomposition

5. _____ is the process used by companies to reduce their costs and increase their profits. Depending on a company's services or Product, the strategies can vary. Every decision in the product development process affects cost.

a. Total cost

b. manufacturing cost

c. Cost reduction

d. Cash flow

1. a
2. d
3. a
4. b
5. c

You can take the complete Chapter Practice Test

for 6. Master Budget and Responsibility Accounting
on all key terms, persons, places, and concepts.

Online 99 Cents

http://www.JustTheFacts101.com

Use www.JustTheFacts101.com for all your study needs

including Facts101's online interactive problem solving labs in

chemistry, statistics, mathematics, and more.

7. Flexible Budgets, Direct-Cost Variances, and Management Control

	Process costing
	Journal entry
	Enterprise resource planning
	Management control
	Performance measurement
	Belief systems
	Benchmarking
	Price variance

CHAPTER HIGHLIGHTS & NOTES: KEY TERMS, PEOPLE, PLACES, CONCEPTS

Process costing	Process costing is a accounting methodology that traces and accumulates direct costs, and allocates indirect costs of a manufacturing process. Costs are assigned to products, usually in a large batch, which might include an entire month's production. Eventually, costs have to be allocated to individual units of product.
Journal entry	A journal entry, in accounting, is a logging of transactions into accounting journal items. The journal entry can consist of several recordings, each of which is either a debit or a credit. The total of the debits must equal the total of the credits or the journal entry is said to be 'unbalanced'.
Enterprise resource planning	Enterprise resource planning is a business management software--usually a suite of integrated applications--that a company can use to store and manage data from every stage of business, including:
	Enterprise resource planning provides an integrated real-time view of core business processes, using common databases maintained by a database management system. Enterprise resource planning systems track business resources--cash, raw materials, production capacity--and the status of business commitments: orders, purchase orders, and payroll.

7. Flexible Budgets, Direct-Cost Variances, and Management Control

Management control	A management control system is a system which gathers and uses information to evaluate the performance of different organizational resources like human, physical, financial and also the organization as a whole considering the organizational strategies. Finally, MCS influences the behavior of organizational resources to implement organizational strategies. MCS might be formal or informal.
Performance measurement	Performance measurement is the process of collecting, analyzing and/or reporting information regarding the performance of an individual, group, organization, system or component. It can involve studying processes/strategies within organizations, or studying engineering processes/parameters/phenomena, to see whether output are in line with what was intended or should have been achieved.
Belief systems	A belief system is a set of mutually supportive beliefs. The beliefs of any such system can be classified as religious, philosophical, ideological, or a combination of these. Philosopher Jonathan Glover says that beliefs are always part of a belief system, and that belief systems are difficult to completely revise.
Benchmarking	Benchmarking is the process of comparing one's business processes and performance metrics to industry bests or best practices from other industries. Dimensions typically measured are quality, time and cost. In the process of best practice benchmarking, management identifies the best firms in their industry, or in another industry where similar processes exist, and compares the results and processes of those studied (the 'targets') to one's own results and processes.
Price variance	The price variance of a material is computed as follows:Vmp = (Actual unit cost - Standard unit cost) * Actual Quantity PurchasedorVmp = (Actual Quantity Purchased * Actual Unit Cost) - (Actual Quantity Purchased * Standard Unit Cost).
	When the Actual Materials Price is higher than the Standard Materials Price, the variance is said to be unfavorable, since the Actual price paid on materials purchased is greater than the allowed standard. The variance is said to be favorable when the Standard materials Price is higher than the Actual Materials Price, since less money was spent in purchasing the materials than the allowed standard.

7. Flexible Budgets, Direct-Cost Variances, and Management Control

1. A _____(s) is a set of mutually supportive beliefs. The beliefs of any such system can be classified as religious, philosophical, ideological, or a combination of these. Philosopher Jonathan Glover says that beliefs are always part of a _____(s), and that _____ are difficult to completely revise.

    a. Consumer Credit Protection Act
    b. Line management
    c. Belief systems
    d. Health Care and Education Reconciliation Act

2. _____ is a accounting methodology that traces and accumulates direct costs, and allocates indirect costs of a manufacturing process. Costs are assigned to products, usually in a large batch, which might include an entire month's production. Eventually, costs have to be allocated to individual units of product.

    a. Process costing
    b. Breakage
    c. Break-even
    d. Constraints accounting

3. _____ is a business management software--usually a suite of integrated applications--that a company can use to store and manage data from every stage of business, including:

    _____ provides an integrated real-time view of core business processes, using common databases maintained by a database management system. _____ systems track business resources--cash, raw materials, production capacity--and the status of business commitments: orders, purchase orders, and payroll. The applications that make up the system share data across the various departments (manufacturing, purchasing, sales, accounting, etc).

    a. Inter Revisjon
    b. Enterprise resource planning
    c. General journal
    d. General ledger

4. . The _____ of a material is computed as follows:Vmp = (Actual unit cost - Standard unit cost) * Actual Quantity PurchasedorVmp = (Actual Quantity Purchased * Actual Unit Cost) - (Actual Quantity Purchased * Standard Unit Cost).

    When the Actual Materials Price is higher than the Standard Materials Price, the variance is said to be unfavorable, since the Actual price paid on materials purchased is greater than the allowed standard. The variance is said to be favorable when the Standard materials Price is higher than the Actual Materials Price, since less money was spent in purchasing the materials than the allowed standard.

    a. Consumer Credit Protection Act
    b. Price variance
    c. Staff management

5. A _____, in accounting, is a logging of transactions into accounting journal items. The _____ can consist of several recordings, each of which is either a debit or a credit. The total of the debits must equal the total of the credits or the _____ is said to be 'unbalanced'.

a. Cash receipts journal
b. Check register
c. General journal
d. Journal entry

1. c

2. a

3. b

4. b

5. d

You can take the complete Chapter Practice Test

for 7. Flexible Budgets, Direct-Cost Variances, and Management Control
on all key terms, persons, places, and concepts.

Online 99 Cents

http://www.JustTheFacts101.com

Use www.JustTheFacts101.com for all your study needs

including Facts101's online interactive problem solving labs in

chemistry, statistics, mathematics, and more.

CHAPTER OUTLINE: KEY TERMS, PEOPLE, PLACES, CONCEPTS

	Fixed cost
	Variable cost
	Cost accounting
	Process costing
	Journal entry
	Activity-based costing

CHAPTER HIGHLIGHTS & NOTES: KEY TERMS, PEOPLE, PLACES, CONCEPTS

Fixed cost	In economics, fixed costs, indirect costs or overheads are business expenses that are not dependent on the level of goods or services produced by the business. They tend to be time-related, such as salaries or rents being paid per month, and are often referred to as overhead costs. This is in contrast to variable costs, which are volume-related (and are paid per quantity produced).
Variable cost	Variable costs are costs that change in proportion to the good or service that a business produces. Variable costs are also the sum of marginal costs over all units produced. They can also be considered normal costs.
Cost accounting	Cost accounting is a complex process of collecting, analyzing, summarizing and evaluating various alternative courses of action. Its goal is to advise the management on the most appropriate course of action based on the cost efficiency and capability. Cost accounting provides the detailed cost information that management needs to control current operations and plan for the future.
Process costing	Process costing is a accounting methodology that traces and accumulates direct costs, and allocates indirect costs of a manufacturing process. Costs are assigned to products, usually in a large batch, which might include an entire month's production. Eventually, costs have to be allocated to individual units of product.
Journal entry	A journal entry, in accounting, is a logging of transactions into accounting journal items. The journal entry can consist of several recordings, each of which is either a debit or a credit.

8. Flexible Budgets, Overhead Cost Variances, and Management Control

Activity-based costing	Activity-based costing is a costing methodology that identifies activities in an organization and assigns the cost of each activity with resources to all products and services according to the actual consumption by each. This model assigns more indirect costs (overhead) into direct costs compared to conventional costing.
	CIMA (Chartered Institute of Management Accountants) defines Activity based costing as an approach to the costing and monitoring of activities which involves tracing resource consumption and costing final outputs.

1. In economics, _____s, indirect costs or overheads are business expenses that are not dependent on the level of goods or services produced by the business. They tend to be time-related, such as salaries or rents being paid per month, and are often referred to as overhead costs. This is in contrast to variable costs, which are volume-related (and are paid per quantity produced).

   a. Backflush accounting
   b. Breakage
   c. Fixed cost
   d. Constraints accounting

2. _____ is a accounting methodology that traces and accumulates direct costs, and allocates indirect costs of a manufacturing process. Costs are assigned to products, usually in a large batch, which might include an entire month's production. Eventually, costs have to be allocated to individual units of product.

   a. Backflush accounting
   b. Breakage
   c. Break-even
   d. Process costing

3. _____s are costs that change in proportion to the good or service that a business produces. _____s are also the sum of marginal costs over all units produced. They can also be considered normal costs.

   a. Backflush accounting
   b. Breakage
   c. Variable cost
   d. Constraints accounting

4. . A _____, in accounting, is a logging of transactions into accounting journal items.

The _____ can consist of several recordings, each of which is either a debit or a credit. The total of the debits must equal the total of the credits or the _____ is said to be 'unbalanced'.

a. Cash receipts journal
b. Check register
c. Journal entry
d. General ledger

5. _____ is a complex process of collecting, analyzing, summarizing and evaluating various alternative courses of action. Its goal is to advise the management on the most appropriate course of action based on the cost efficiency and capability. _____ provides the detailed cost information that management needs to control current operations and plan for the future.

a. Backflush accounting
b. Cost accounting
c. Break-even
d. Constraints accounting

1. c
2. d
3. c
4. c
5. b

You can take the complete Chapter Practice Test

for 8. Flexible Budgets, Overhead Cost Variances, and Management Control
on all key terms, persons, places, and concepts.

Online 99 Cents

http://www.JustTheFacts101.com

Use www.JustTheFacts101.com for all your study needs

including Facts101's online interactive problem solving labs in

chemistry, statistics, mathematics, and more.

9. Inventory Costing and Capacity Analysis

	Variable Costing
	Absorption Costing
	Operating income
	Process costing
	Performance measurement
	Capacity utilization
	Manufacturing cost
	Capacity management
	Fixed cost
	Activity-based costing

CHAPTER HIGHLIGHTS & NOTES: KEY TERMS, PEOPLE, PLACES, CONCEPTS

Variable Costing	Variable Costing is a managerial accounting cost concept. Under this method, manufacturing overhead is incurred in the period that a product is produced. This addresses the issue of absorption costing that allows income to rise as production rises.
Absorption Costing	Total absorption costing is a method of Accounting cost which entails the full cost of manufacturing or providing a service. TAC includes not just the costs of materials and labour, but also of all manufacturing overheads (whether 'fixed' or 'variable').The cost of each cost center can be direct or indirect cost. The direct cost can be easily identified with individual cost centers.
Operating income	In accounting and finance, earnings before interest and taxes, is a measure of a firm's profit that excludes interest and income tax expenses. It Is the difference between operating revenues and operating expenses. When a firm does not have non-operating income, then operating income is sometimes used as a synonym for EBIT and operating profit.

9. Inventory Costing and Capacity Analysis

Process costing	Process costing is a accounting methodology that traces and accumulates direct costs, and allocates indirect costs of a manufacturing process. Costs are assigned to products, usually in a large batch, which might include an entire month's production. Eventually, costs have to be allocated to individual units of product.
Performance measurement	Performance measurement is the process of collecting, analyzing and/or reporting information regarding the performance of an individual, group, organization, system or component. It can involve studying processes/strategies within organizations, or studying engineering processes/parameters/phenomena, to see whether output are in line with what was intended or should have been achieved.
Capacity utilization	Capacity utilization is the extent to which an enterprise or a nation actually uses its installed productive capacity. It is the relationship between actual output that 'is' actually produced with the installed equipment, and the potential output which 'could' be produced with it, if capacity was fully used.
Manufacturing cost	Manufacturing cost is the sum of costs of all resources consumed in the process of making a product. The manufacturing cost is classified into three categories: direct materials cost, direct labor cost and manufacturing overhead.
Capacity management	Capacity management is a process used to manage information technology . Its primary goal is to ensure that IT capacity meets current and future business requirements in a cost-effective manner. One common interpretation of capacity management is described in the ITIL framework.
Fixed cost	In economics, fixed costs, indirect costs or overheads are business expenses that are not dependent on the level of goods or services produced by the business. They tend to be time-related, such as salaries or rents being paid per month, and are often referred to as overhead costs. This is in contrast to variable costs, which are volume-related (and are paid per quantity produced).
Activity-based costing	Activity-based costing is a costing methodology that identifies activities in an organization and assigns the cost of each activity with resources to all products and services according to the actual consumption by each. This model assigns more indirect costs (overhead) into direct costs compared to conventional costing. CIMA (Chartered Institute of Management Accountants) defines Activity based costing as an approach to the costing and monitoring of activities which involves tracing resource consumption and costing final outputs.

9. Inventory Costing and Capacity Analysis

1. In accounting and finance, earnings before interest and taxes, is a measure of a firm's profit that excludes interest and income tax expenses. It is the difference between operating revenues and operating expenses. When a firm does not have non-_____, then _____ is sometimes used as a synonym for EBIT and operating profit.

    a. Operating income
    b. Bachelor tax
    c. BDO International
    d. Big Four

2. _____ is a accounting methodology that traces and accumulates direct costs, and allocates indirect costs of a manufacturing process. Costs are assigned to products, usually in a large batch, which might include an entire month's production. Eventually, costs have to be allocated to individual units of product.

    a. Backflush accounting
    b. Breakage
    c. Process costing
    d. Constraints accounting

3. _____ is a costing methodology that identifies activities in an organization and assigns the cost of each activity with resources to all products and services according to the actual consumption by each. This model assigns more indirect costs (overhead) into direct costs compared to conventional costing.

    CIMA (Chartered Institute of Management Accountants) defines Activity based costing as an approach to the costing and monitoring of activities which involves tracing resource consumption and costing final outputs.

    a. Managerial risk accounting
    b. Variable Costing
    c. Bachelor tax
    d. Activity-based costing

4. Total _____ is a method of Accounting cost which entails the full cost of manufacturing or providing a service. TAC includes not just the costs of materials and labour, but also of all manufacturing overheads (whether 'fixed' or 'variable').The cost of each cost center can be direct or indirect cost. The direct cost can be easily identified with individual cost centers.

    a. Inter Revisjon
    b. Bachelor tax
    c. Absorption Costing
    d. Big Four

5. . _____ is the extent to which an enterprise or a nation actually uses its installed productive capacity. It is the relationship between actual output that 'is' actually produced with the installed equipment, and the potential output which 'could' be produced with it, if capacity was fully used.

    a. Consumer Credit Protection Act

b. Line management

c. Capacity utilization

d. Health Care and Education Reconciliation Act

1. a

2. c

3. d

4. c

5. c

You can take the complete Chapter Practice Test

for 9. Inventory Costing and Capacity Analysis
on all key terms, persons, places, and concepts.

Online 99 Cents

http://www.JustTheFacts101.com

Use www.JustTheFacts101.com for all your study needs

including Facts101's online interactive problem solving labs in

chemistry, statistics, mathematics, and more.

10. Determining How Costs Behave

CHAPTER OUTLINE: KEY TERMS, PEOPLE, PLACES, CONCEPTS

_____ Estimation

_____ Cost object

_____ Time horizon

_____ Cost driver

_____ Cash flow

_____ Decision-making process

_____ Industrial engineering

_____ Cross-sectional data

_____ Standard error

_____ Goodness of fit

_____ Activity-based costing

_____ Experience curve

_____ Regression Analysis

_____ Coefficient of determination

_____ Confidence interval

_____ Autocorrelation

_____ Error term

_____ Heteroscedasticity

_____ Multicollinearity

10. Determining How Costs Behave

Estimation	Estimation is the process of finding an estimate, or approximation, which is a value that is usable for some purpose even if input data may be incomplete, uncertain, or unstable. The value is nonetheless usable because it is derived from the best information available. Typically, estimation involves 'using the value of a statistic derived from a sample to estimate the value of a corresponding population parameter'.
Cost object	A cost object is a tangible input for a product manufactured/service provided, like labor or material. For example a cloth manufacturing firm requires some amount of predetermined labor and predetermined raw material for any amount of cloth being manufactured. The cost of employing labor can be directly fixed as 'per man per hour' or 'per man per day per hour per minute per annum', so the labor is a cost object as you can directly associate cost with it.
Time horizon	A time horizon, also known as a planning horizon, is a fixed point of time in the future at which point certain processes will be evaluated or assumed to end. It is necessary in an accounting, finance or risk management regime to assign such a fixed horizon time so that alternatives can be evaluated for performance over the same period of time. A time horizon is a physical impossibility in the real world.
Cost driver	According to CIMA, 'cost driver is any factor which causes a change in the cost of an activity. A cost driver is the unit of an activity that causes the change in activity's cost. Examples: In marketing, cost drivers are Number of advertisements, Number of sales personnel etc.
Cash flow	Cash flow is the movement of money into or out of a business, project, or financial product. It is usually measured during a specified, limited period of time. Measurement of cash flow can be used for calculating other parameters that give information on a company's value and situation.
Decision-making process	Decision-making can be regarded as the cognitive process resulting in the selection of a belief or a course of action among several alternative possibilities. Every decision-making process produces a final choice that may or may not prompt action. Decision making is one of the central activities of management and is a huge part of any process of implementation.
Industrial engineering	Industrial engineering is a branch of engineering dealing with the optimization of complex processes or systems. It is concerned with the development, improvement, implementation and evaluation of integrated systems of people, money, knowledge, information, equipment, energy, materials, analysis and synthesis, as well as the mathematical, physical and social sciences together with the principles and methods of engineering design to specify, predict, and evaluate the results to be obtained from such systems or processes. Its underlying concepts overlap considerably with certain business-oriented disciplines such as operations management.
Cross-sectional data	Cross-sectional data, or a cross section of a study population, in statistics and econometrics is a type of one-dimensional data set.

	Cross-sectional data refers to data collected by observing many subjects (such as individuals, firms or countries/regions) at the same point of time, or without regard to differences in time. Analysis of cross-sectional data usually consists of comparing the differences among the subjects.
Standard error	The standard error is the standard deviation of the sampling distribution of a statistic. The term may also be used to refer to an estimate of that standard deviation, derived from a particular sample used to compute the estimate. For example, the sample mean is the usual estimator of a population mean.
Goodness of fit	The goodness of fit of a statistical model describes how well it fits a set of observations. Measures of goodness of fit typically summarize the discrepancy between observed values and the values expected under the model in question. Such measures can be used in statistical hypothesis testing, e.g. to test for normality of residuals, to test whether two samples are drawn from identical distributions, or whether outcome frequencies follow a specified distribution .
Activity-based costing	Activity-based costing is a costing methodology that identifies activities in an organization and assigns the cost of each activity with resources to all products and services according to the actual consumption by each. This model assigns more indirect costs (overhead) into direct costs compared to conventional costing. CIMA (Chartered Institute of Management Accountants) defines Activity based costing as an approach to the costing and monitoring of activities which involves tracing resource consumption and costing final outputs.
Experience curve	In management, models of the learning curve effect and the closely related experience curve effect express the relationship between equations for experience and efficiency or between efficiency gains and investment in the effort.
Regression Analysis	In statistics, regression analysis is a statistical process for estimating the relationships among variables. It includes many techniques for modeling and analyzing several variables, when the focus is on the relationship between a dependent variable and one or more independent variables. More specifically, regression analysis helps one understand how the typical value of the dependent variable (or 'Criterion Variable') changes when any one of the independent variables is varied, while the other independent variables are held fixed.
Coefficient of determination	In statistics, the coefficient of determination, denoted R^2 and pronounced R squared, indicates how well data points fit a statistical model - sometimes simply a line or curve. It is a statistic used in the context of statistical models whose main purpose is either the prediction of future outcomes or the testing of hypotheses, on the basis of other related information.

10. Determining How Costs Behave

Confidence interval	In statistics, a confidence interval is a type of interval estimate of a population parameter and is used to indicate the reliability of an estimate. It is an observed interval (i.e. it is calculated from the observations), in principle different from sample to sample, that frequently includes the parameter of interest if the experiment is repeated. How frequently the observed interval contains the parameter is determined by the confidence level or confidence coefficient.
Autocorrelation	Autocorrelation is the cross-correlation of a signal with itself. Informally, it is the similarity between observations as a function of the time lag between them. It is a mathematical tool for finding repeating patterns, such as the presence of a periodic signal obscured by noise, or identifying the missing fundamental frequency in a signal implied by its harmonic frequencies.
Error term	An error term is an additive type of error. Common examples include:•errors and residuals in statistics, e.g. in linear regression•the error term in numerical integration.
Heteroscedasticity	In statistics, a collection of random variables is heteroscedastic if there are sub-populations that have different variabilities from others. Here 'variability' could be quantified by the variance or any other measure of statistical dispersion. Thus heteroscedasticity is the absence of homoscedasticity.
Multicollinearity	Multicollinearity is a statistical phenomenon in which two or more predictor variables in a multiple regression model are highly correlated, meaning that one can be linearly predicted from the others with a non-trivial degree of accuracy. In this situation the coefficient estimates of the multiple regression may change erratically in response to small changes in the model or the data. Multicollinearity does not reduce the predictive power or reliability of the model as a whole, at least within the sample data themselves; it only affects calculations regarding individual predictors.

1. In statistics, a _____ is a type of interval estimate of a population parameter and is used to indicate the reliability of an estimate. It is an observed interval (i.e. it is calculated from the observations), in principle different from sample to sample, that frequently includes the parameter of interest if the experiment is repeated. How frequently the observed interval contains the parameter is determined by the confidence level or confidence coefficient.

   a. Confidence interval
   b. Health Care and Education Reconciliation Act
   c. Social Security Act
   d. BDO International

2. _____ is the process of finding an estimate, or approximation, which is a value that is usable for some purpose even if input data may be incomplete, uncertain, or unstable. The value is nonetheless usable because it is derived from the best information available. Typically, _____ involves 'using the value of a statistic derived from a sample to estimate the value of a corresponding population parameter'.

   a. Inter Revisjon
   b. Estimation
   c. Accredited Business Accountant
   d. Indian Chartered Accountancy Course

3. A _____ is a tangible input for a product manufactured/service provided, like labor or material. For example a cloth manufacturing firm requires some amount of predetermined labor and predetermined raw material for any amount of cloth being manufactured. The cost of employing labor can be directly fixed as 'per man per hour' or 'per man per day per hour per minute per annum', so the labor is a _____ as you can directly associate cost with it.

   a. Consumer Credit Protection Act
   b. Cost object
   c. Social Security Act
   d. Bachelor tax

4. A _____, also known as a planning horizon, is a fixed point of time in the future at which point certain processes will be evaluated or assumed to end. It is necessary in an accounting, finance or risk management regime to assign such a fixed horizon time so that alternatives can be evaluated for performance over the same period of time. A _____ is a physical impossibility in the real world.

   a. Consumer Credit Protection Act
   b. Health Care and Education Reconciliation Act
   c. Social Security Act
   d. Time horizon

5. According to CIMA, '_____ is any factor which causes a change in the cost of an activity. A _____ is the unit of an activity that causes the change in activity's cost. Examples: In marketing, _____s are Number of advertisements, Number of sales personnel etc.

   a. Cost driver
   b. Breakage
   c. Break-even
   d. Constraints accounting

1. a
2. b
3. b
4. d
5. a

You can take the complete Chapter Practice Test

for 10. Determining How Costs Behave
on all key terms, persons, places, and concepts.

Online 99 Cents

http://www.JustTheFacts101.com

Use www.JustTheFacts101.com for all your study needs

including Facts101's online interactive problem solving labs in

chemistry, statistics, mathematics, and more.

11. Decision Making and Relevant Information

CVP analysis

Decision-making process

Relevant cost

Sunk cost

Cost reduction

Job costing

Insourcing

Outsourcing

Opportunity cost

Carrying cost

Book value

Theory of Constraints

Value theory

Customer profitability

Linear programming

Objective function

Sensitivity analysis

11. Decision Making and Relevant Information

CVP analysis	Cost-volume-profit, in managerial economics, is a form of cost accounting. It is a simplified model, useful for elementary instruction and for short-run decisions. CVP analysis expands the use of information provided by breakeven analysis.
Decision-making process	Decision-making can be regarded as the cognitive process resulting in the selection of a belief or a course of action among several alternative possibilities. Every decision-making process produces a final choice that may or may not prompt action. Decision making is one of the central activities of management and is a huge part of any process of implementation.
Relevant cost	A relevant cost is a cost that differs between alternatives being considered. It is often important for businesses to distinguish between relevant and irrelevant costs when analyzing alternatives because erroneously considering irrelevant costs can lead to unsound business decisions. Also, ignoring irrelevant data in analysis can save time and effort.
Sunk cost	In economics and business decision-making, a sunk cost is a retrospective cost that has already been incurred and cannot be recovered. Sunk costs are sometimes contrasted with prospective costs, which are future costs that may be incurred or changed if an action is taken. Both retrospective and prospective costs may be either fixed (continuous for as long as the business is in operation and unaffected by output volume) or variable (dependent on volume) costs.
Cost reduction	Cost reduction is the process used by companies to reduce their costs and increase their profits. Depending on a company's services or Product, the strategies can vary. Every decision in the product development process affects cost.
Job costing	Job Costing involves the calculation of costs involved in a construction 'job' or the manufacturing of goods done in discrete batches. These costs are recorded in ledger accounts throughout the life of the job or batch and are then summarized in the final trial balance before the preparing of the job cost or batch manufacturing statement.
Insourcing	Insourcing is the cessation by a company of contracting a business function and the commencement of performing it internally. Insourcing is the opposite of outsourcing. Insourcing is a business decision that is often made to maintain control of critical production or competencies.
Outsourcing	In business, outsourcing is the contracting out of a business process to a third-party. The term 'outsourcing' became popular in the United States near the turn of the 21st century. Outsourcing sometimes involves transferring employees and assets from one firm to another, but not always.
Opportunity cost	In microeconomic theory, the opportunity cost of a choice is the value of the best alternative forgone, in a situation in which a choice needs to be made between several mutually exclusive alternatives given limited resources. Assuming the best choice is made, it is the 'cost' incurred by not enjoying the benefit that would be had by taking the second best choice available.

11. Decision Making and Relevant Information

Carrying cost	In marketing, carrying cost refers to the total cost of holding inventory. This includes warehousing costs such as rent, utilities and salaries, financial costs such as opportunity cost, and inventory costs related to perishability, pilferage, shrinkage and insurance. When there are no transaction costs for shipment, carrying costs are minimized when no excess inventory is held at all, as in a Just In Time production system.
Book value	In accounting, book value or carrying value is the value of an asset according to its balance sheet account balance. For assets, the value is based on the original cost of the asset less any depreciation, amortization or impairment costs made against the asset. Traditionally, a company's book value is its total assets minus intangible assets and liabilities.
Theory of Constraints	The theory of constraints is a management paradigm that views any manageable system as being limited in achieving more of its goals by a very small number of constraints. There is always at least one constraint, and Theory of Constraints uses a focusing process to identify the constraint and restructure the rest of the organization around it. Theory of Constraints adopts the common idiom 'a chain is no stronger than its weakest link.' This means that processes, organizations, etc., are vulnerable because the weakest person or part can always damage or break them or at least adversely affect the outcome.
Value theory	Value theory encompasses a range of approaches to understanding how, why and to what degree people value things; whether the thing is a person, idea, object, or anything else. This investigation began in ancient philosophy, where it is called axiology or ethics. Early philosophical investigations sought to understand good and evil and the concept of 'the good'.
Customer profitability	Customer profitability is the profit the firm makes from serving a customer or customer group over a specified period of time, specifically the difference between the revenues earned from and the costs associated with the customer relationship in a specified period. According to Philip Kotler,'a profitable customer is a person, household or a company that overtime, yields a revenue stream that exceeds by an acceptable amount the company's cost stream of attracting, selling and servicing the customer.' Calculating customer profit is an important step in understanding which customer relationships are better than others. Often, the firm will find that some customer relationships are unprofitable.
Linear programming	Linear programming is a method to achieve the best outcome (such as maximum profit or lowest cost) in a mathematical model whose requirements are represented by linear relationships. Linear programming is a special case of mathematical programming (mathematical optimization).

11. Decision Making and Relevant Information

Objective function	In mathematical optimization, statistics, decision theory and machine learning, a loss function or cost function is a function that maps an event or values of one or more variables onto a real number intuitively representing some 'cost' associated with the event. An optimization problem seeks to minimize a loss function. An objective function is either a loss function or its negative (sometimes called a reward function or a utility function), in which case it is to be maximized.
Sensitivity analysis	Sensitivity analysis is the study of how the uncertainty in the output of a mathematical model or system can be apportioned to different sources of uncertainty in its inputs. A related practice is uncertainty analysis, which has a greater focus on uncertainty quantification and propagation of uncertainty. Ideally, uncertainty and sensitivity analysis should be run in tandem.

CHAPTER QUIZ: KEY TERMS, PEOPLE, PLACES, CONCEPTS

1. Decision-making can be regarded as the cognitive process resulting in the selection of a belief or a course of action among several alternative possibilities. Every _____ produces a final choice that may or may not prompt action. Decision making is one of the central activities of management and is a huge part of any process of implementation.

   a. Decision-making process
   b. Health Care and Education Reconciliation Act
   c. Social Security Act
   d. Bachelor tax

2. _____ is the cessation by a company of contracting a business function and the commencement of performing it internally. _____ is the opposite of outsourcing. _____ is a business decision that is often made to maintain control of critical production or competencies.

   a. Inter Revisjon
   b. Insourcing
   c. Break-even
   d. Constraints accounting

3. . In microeconomic theory, the _____ of a choice is the value of the best alternative forgone, in a situation in which a choice needs to be made between several mutually exclusive alternatives given limited resources. Assuming the best choice is made, it is the 'cost' incurred by not enjoying the benefit that would be had by taking the second best choice available. The New Oxford American Dictionary defines it as 'the loss of potential gain from other alternatives when one alternative is chosen'.

   a. Inter Revisjon

b. Breakage

c. Opportunity cost

d. Constraints accounting

4. _____ is the profit the firm makes from serving a customer or customer group over a specified period of time, specifically the difference between the revenues earned from and the costs associated with the customer relationship in a specified period. According to Philip Kotler,'a profitable customer is a person, household or a company that overtime, yields a revenue stream that exceeds by an acceptable amount the company's cost stream of attracting, selling and servicing the customer.'

Calculating customer profit is an important step in understanding which customer relationships are better than others. Often, the firm will find that some customer relationships are unprofitable.

a. Backflush accounting

b. Breakage

c. Break-even

d. Customer profitability

5. _____ is the process used by companies to reduce their costs and increase their profits. Depending on a company's services or Product, the strategies can vary. Every decision in the product development process affects cost.

a. Total cost

b. manufacturing cost

c. Cost reduction

d. Constraints accounting

ANSWER KEY
11. Decision Making and Relevant Information

1. a
2. b
3. c
4. d
5. c

You can take the complete Chapter Practice Test

for 11. Decision Making and Relevant Information
on all key terms, persons, places, and concepts.

Online 99 Cents

http://www.JustTheFacts101.com

Use www.JustTheFacts101.com for all your study needs

including Facts101's online interactive problem solving labs in

chemistry, statistics, mathematics, and more.

12. Strategy, Balanced Scorecard, and Strategic Profitability Analysis

CHAPTER OUTLINE: KEY TERMS, PEOPLE, PLACES, CONCEPTS

	Bargaining power
	Cost leadership
	Product differentiation
	Balanced Scorecard
	Triple bottom line
	Operating income
	Cost driver
	Productivity
	Decision-making process
	Ending inventory
	Partial productivity
	Total factor productivity

CHAPTER HIGHLIGHTS & NOTES: KEY TERMS, PEOPLE, PLACES, CONCEPTS

Bargaining power	Bargaining power is the relative ability of parties in a situation to exert influence over each other. If both parties are on an equal footing in a debate, then they will have equal bargaining power, such as in a perfectly competitive market, or between an evenly matched monopoly and monopsony. There are a number of fields where the concept of bargaining power has proven crucial to coherent analysis: game theory, labour economics, collective bargaining arrangements, diplomatic negotiations, settlement of litigation, the price of insurance, and any negotiation in general.
Cost leadership	Cost leadership is a concept developed by Michael Porter, used in business strategy. It describes a way to establish the competitive advantage.

12. Strategy, Balanced Scorecard, and Strategic Profitability Analysis

Product differentiation	In economics and marketing, product differentiation is the process of distinguishing a product or service from others, to make it more attractive to a particular target market. This involves differentiating it from competitors' products as well as a firm's own products. The concept was proposed by Edward Chamberlin in his 1933 Theory of Monopolistic Competition.
Balanced Scorecard	The balanced scorecard is a strategy performance management tool - a semi-standard structured report, supported by design methods and automation tools, that can be used by managers to keep track of the execution of activities by the staff within their control and to monitor the consequences arising from these actions. It is perhaps the best known of several such frameworks (it was the most widely adopted performance management framework reported in the 2010 annual survey of management tools undertaken by Bain & Company)..
Triple bottom line	Triple bottom line incorporates the notion of sustainability into business decisions. The Triple bottom line is an accounting framework with three dimensions: social, environmental (or ecological) and financial. The Triple bottom line dimensions are also commonly called the three Ps: people, planet and profits and are referred to as the 'three pillars of sustainability.' Interest in triple bottom line accounting has been growing in both for-profit, nonprofit and government sectors.
Operating income	In accounting and finance, earnings before interest and taxes, is a measure of a firm's profit that excludes interest and income tax expenses. It is the difference between operating revenues and operating expenses. When a firm does not have non-operating income, then operating income is sometimes used as a synonym for EBIT and operating profit.
Cost driver	According to CIMA, 'cost driver is any factor which causes a change in the cost of an activity. A cost driver is the unit of an activity that causes the change in activity's cost. Examples: In marketing, cost drivers are Number of advertisements, Number of sales personnel etc.
Productivity	Productivity is the ratio of output to inputs in production; it is an average measure of the efficiency of production. Efficiency of production means production's capability to create incomes which is measured by the formula real output value minus real input value. Increasing national productivity can raise living standards because more real income improves people's ability to purchase goods and services, enjoy leisure, improve housing and education and contribute to social and environmental programs.
Decision-making process	Decision-making can be regarded as the cognitive process resulting in the selection of a belief or a course of action among several alternative possibilities. Every decision-making process produces a final choice that may or may not prompt action. Decision making is one of the central activities of management and is a huge part of any process of implementation.
Ending inventory	Ending inventory is the amount of inventory a company has in stock at the end of its fiscal year.

	It is closely related with ending inventory cost, which is the amount of money spent to get these goods in stock. It should be calculated at the lower of cost or market.
Partial productivity	Measurement of partial productivity refers to the measurement solutions which do not meet the requirements of total productivity measurement, yet, being practicable as indicators of total productivity. In practice, measurement in production means measures of partial productivity. In that case, the objects of measurement are components of total productivity, and interpreted correctly, these components are indicative of productivity development.
Total factor productivity	In economics, total-factor productivity, also called multi-factor productivity, is a variable which accounts for effects in total output not caused by traditionally measured inputs of labor and capital. If all inputs are accounted for, then total factor productivity can be taken as a measure of an economy's long-term technological change or technological dynamism. total factor productivity cannot be measured directly.

CHAPTER QUIZ: KEY TERMS, PEOPLE, PLACES, CONCEPTS

1. _____ is the relative ability of parties in a situation to exert influence over each other. If both parties are on an equal footing in a debate, then they will have equal _____, such as in a perfectly competitive market, or between an evenly matched monopoly and monopsony.

   There are a number of fields where the concept of _____ has proven crucial to coherent analysis: game theory, labour economics, collective bargaining arrangements, diplomatic negotiations, settlement of litigation, the price of insurance, and any negotiation in general.

   a. Consumer Credit Protection Act
   b. Health Care and Education Reconciliation Act
   c. Social Security Act
   d. Bargaining power

2. . According to CIMA, '_____ is any factor which causes a change in the cost of an activity. A _____ is the unit of an activity that causes the change in activity's cost. Examples: In marketing, _____s are Number of advertisements, Number of sales personnel etc.

   a. Backflush accounting
   b. Breakage
   c. Cost driver

3. In economics and marketing, _____ is the process of distinguishing a product or service from others, to make it more attractive to a particular target market. This involves differentiating it from competitors' products as well as a firm's own products. The concept was proposed by Edward Chamberlin in his 1933 Theory of Monopolistic Competition.

   a. Consumer Credit Protection Act
   b. Health Care and Education Reconciliation Act
   c. Social Security Act
   d. Product differentiation

4. Decision-making can be regarded as the cognitive process resulting in the selection of a belief or a course of action among several alternative possibilities. Every _____ produces a final choice that may or may not prompt action. Decision making is one of the central activities of management and is a huge part of any process of implementation.

   a. Decision-making process
   b. Breakage
   c. Break-even
   d. Constraints accounting

5. _____ is a concept developed by Michael Porter, used in business strategy. It describes a way to establish the competitive advantage. _____, in basic words, means the lowest cost of operation in the industry.

   a. Consumer Credit Protection Act
   b. Cost leadership
   c. Social Security Act
   d. Bachelor tax

1. d
2. c
3. d
4. a
5. b

You can take the complete Chapter Practice Test

for 12. Strategy, Balanced Scorecard, and Strategic Profitability Analysis
on all key terms, persons, places, and concepts.

Online 99 Cents

http://www.JustTheFacts101.com

Use www.JustTheFacts101.com for all your study needs

including Facts101's online interactive problem solving labs in

chemistry, statistics, mathematics, and more.

13. Pricing Decisions and Cost Management

CHAPTER OUTLINE: KEY TERMS, PEOPLE, PLACES, CONCEPTS

	Cost allocation
	Long run
	Operating income
	Sustainability
	Bargaining power
	Competitor analysis
	Target costing
	Cost reduction
	Value engineering
	Productivity
	Cost-plus pricing
	Peak-load pricing
	Federal Trade Commission Act
	Predatory pricing

13. Pricing Decisions and Cost Management

Cost allocation	Cost allocation is a process of providing relief to shared service organization's cost centers that provide a product or service. In turn, the associated expense is assigned to internal clients' cost centers that consume the products and services. For example, the CIO may provide all IT services within the company and assign the costs back to the business units that consume each offering.
Long run	In microeconomics, the long run is the conceptual time period in which there are no fixed factors of production as to changing the output level by changing the capital stock or by entering or leaving an industry. The long run contrasts with the short run, in which some factors are variable and others are fixed, constraining entry or exit from an industry. In macroeconomics, the long run is the period when the general price level, contractual wage rates, and expectations adjust fully to the state of the economy, in contrast to the short run when these variables may not fully adjust.
Operating income	In accounting and finance, earnings before interest and taxes, is a measure of a firm's profit that excludes interest and income tax expenses. It is the difference between operating revenues and operating expenses. When a firm does not have non-operating income, then operating income is sometimes used as a synonym for EBIT and operating profit.
Sustainability	In ecology, sustainability is how biological systems endure and remain diverse and productive. Long-lived and healthy wetlands and forests are examples of sustainable biological systems. In more general terms, sustainability refers to the endurance of systems and processes.
Bargaining power	Bargaining power is the relative ability of parties in a situation to exert influence over each other. If both parties are on an equal footing in a debate, then they will have equal bargaining power, such as in a perfectly competitive market, or between an evenly matched monopoly and monopsony. There are a number of fields where the concept of bargaining power has proven crucial to coherent analysis: game theory, labour economics, collective bargaining arrangements, diplomatic negotiations, settlement of litigation, the price of insurance, and any negotiation in general.
Competitor analysis	Competitor analysis in marketing and strategic management is an assessment of the strengths and weaknesses of current and potential competitors. This analysis provides both an offensive and defensive strategic context to identify opportunities and threats. Profiling coalesces all of the relevant sources of competitor analysis into one framework in the support of efficient and effective strategy formulation, implementation, monitoring and adjustment.
Target costing	Target costing is a pricing method used by firms. It is defined as 'a cost management tool for reducing the overall cost of a product over its entire life-cycle with the help of production, engineering, research and design'. A target cost is the maximum amount of cost that can be incurred on a product and with it the firm can still earn the required profit margin from that product at a particular selling price.
Cost reduction	Cost reduction is the process used by companies to reduce their costs and increase their profits.

	Depending on a company's services or Product, the strategies can vary. Every decision in the product development process affects cost.
Value engineering	Value engineering is a systematic method to improve the 'value' of goods or products and services by using an examination of function. Value, as defined, is the ratio of function to cost. Value can therefore be increased by either improving the function or reducing the cost.
Productivity	Productivity is the ratio of output to inputs in production; it is an average measure of the efficiency of production. Efficiency of production means production's capability to create incomes which is measured by the formula real output value minus real input value.
	Increasing national productivity can raise living standards because more real income improves people's ability to purchase goods and services, enjoy leisure, improve housing and education and contribute to social and environmental programs.
Cost-plus pricing	Cost-plus pricing is a pricing strategy companies use to maximize their rates of return.
	Firms may accomplish their objective of profit maximization by increasing their production until marginal revenue equals marginal cost and then charging a price which is determined by the demand curve. However, in practice, most firms use either value-based pricing or cost-plus pricing which is also known as mark-up pricing.
Peak-load pricing	Peak-load pricing is a pricing technique applied to public goods, which is a particular case of a Lindahl equilibrium. Instead of different demands for the same public good, we consider the demands for a public good in different periods of the day, month or year, then finding the optimal capacity (quantity supplied) and, afterwards, the optimal peak-load prices.
	This has particular applications in public goods such as public urban transportation, where day demand (peak period) is usually much higher than night demand (off-peak period).
Federal Trade Commission Act	The Federal Trade Commission Act of 1914 (FTC Act) established the Federal Trade Commission (FTC). As initially established it consisted of a bipartisan body of five members appointed by the president of the United States for seven-year terms.
	The FTC Act was one of President Woodrow Wilson's major acts against trusts, and the Clayton Antitrust Act would be signed three weeks later.
Predatory pricing	Predatory pricing is a pricing strategy where a product or service is set at a very low price, intending to drive competitors out of the market, or create barriers to entry for potential new competitors. If competitors or potential competitors cannot sustain equal or lower prices without losing money, they go out of business or choose not to enter the business.

13. Pricing Decisions and Cost Management

1. _____ is a pricing strategy where a product or service is set at a very low price, intending to drive competitors out of the market, or create barriers to entry for potential new competitors. If competitors or potential competitors cannot sustain equal or lower prices without losing money, they go out of business or choose not to enter the business. The predatory merchant then has fewer competitors or is even a de facto monopoly.

   a. Consumer Credit Protection Act
   b. Predatory pricing
   c. Health Care and Education Reconciliation Act
   d. Constraints accounting

2. _____ is the relative ability of parties in a situation to exert influence over each other. If both parties are on an equal footing in a debate, then they will have equal _____, such as in a perfectly competitive market, or between an evenly matched monopoly and monopsony.

   There are a number of fields where the concept of _____ has proven crucial to coherent analysis: game theory, labour economics, collective bargaining arrangements, diplomatic negotiations, settlement of litigation, the price of insurance, and any negotiation in general.

   a. Consumer Credit Protection Act
   b. total factor productivity
   c. capacity utilization
   d. Bargaining power

3. In microeconomics, the _____ is the conceptual time period in which there are no fixed factors of production as to changing the output level by changing the capital stock or by entering or leaving an industry. The _____ contrasts with the short run, in which some factors are variable and others are fixed, constraining entry or exit from an industry. In macroeconomics, the _____ is the period when the general price level, contractual wage rates, and expectations adjust fully to the state of the economy, in contrast to the short run when these variables may not fully adjust.

   a. Partial productivity
   b. total factor productivity
   c. Long run
   d. Consumer Credit Protection Act

4. _____ is a systematic method to improve the 'value' of goods or products and services by using an examination of function. Value, as defined, is the ratio of function to cost. Value can therefore be increased by either improving the function or reducing the cost.

   a. Value engineering
   b. manufacturing cost
   c. Health Care and Education Reconciliation Act
   d. Constraints accounting

5. _____ is a process of providing relief to shared service organization's cost centers that provide a product or service. In turn, the associated expense is assigned to internal clients' cost centers that consume the products and services. For example, the CIO may provide all IT services within the company and assign the costs back to the business units that consume each offering.

a. Bank examiner
b. Bookkeeping
c. Cost allocation
d. Carbon accounting

1. b

2. d

3. c

4. a

5. c

You can take the complete Chapter Practice Test

for 13. Pricing Decisions and Cost Management
on all key terms, persons, places, and concepts.

Online 99 Cents

http://www.JustTheFacts101.com

Use www.JustTheFacts101.com for all your study needs

including Facts101's online interactive problem solving labs in

chemistry, statistics, mathematics, and more.

14. Cost Allocation, Customer-Profitability Analysis, and Sales Variance A

CHAPTER OUTLINE: KEY TERMS, PEOPLE, PLACES, CONCEPTS

_____	Cost reduction
_____	Decision-making process
_____	Operating income
_____	Cost allocation
_____	CVP analysis
_____	Process costing

CHAPTER HIGHLIGHTS & NOTES: KEY TERMS, PEOPLE, PLACES, CONCEPTS

Cost reduction	Cost reduction is the process used by companies to reduce their costs and increase their profits. Depending on a company's services or Product, the strategies can vary. Every decision in the product development process affects cost.
Decision-making process	Decision-making can be regarded as the cognitive process resulting in the selection of a belief or a course of action among several alternative possibilities. Every decision-making process produces a final choice that may or may not prompt action. Decision making is one of the central activities of management and is a huge part of any process of implementation.
Operating income	In accounting and finance, earnings before interest and taxes, is a measure of a firm's profit that excludes interest and income tax expenses. It is the difference between operating revenues and operating expenses. When a firm does not have non-operating income, then operating income is sometimes used as a synonym for EBIT and operating profit.
Cost allocation	Cost allocation is a process of providing relief to shared service organization's cost centers that provide a product or service. In turn, the associated expense is assigned to internal clients' cost centers that consume the products and services. For example, the CIO may provide all IT services within the company and assign the costs back to the business units that consume each offering.
CVP analysis	Cost-volume-profit, in managerial economics, is a form of cost accounting. It is a simplified model, useful for elementary instruction and for short-run decisions.

Process costing	Process costing is a accounting methodology that traces and accumulates direct costs, and allocates indirect costs of a manufacturing process. Costs are assigned to products, usually in a large batch, which might include an entire month's production. Eventually, costs have to be allocated to individual units of product.

1. Cost-volume-profit, in managerial economics, is a form of cost accounting. It is a simplified model, useful for elementary instruction and for short-run decisions.

   _____ expands the use of information provided by breakeven analysis.

   a. Consumer Credit Protection Act
   b. CVP analysis
   c. Business mileage reimbursement rate
   d. Carbon accounting

2. In accounting and finance, earnings before interest and taxes, is a measure of a firm's profit that excludes interest and income tax expenses. It is the difference between operating revenues and operating expenses. When a firm does not have non-_____, then _____ is sometimes used as a synonym for EBIT and operating profit.

   a. Inter Revisjon
   b. manufacturing cost
   c. Operating income
   d. Accredited Business Accountant

3. _____ is a process of providing relief to shared service organization's cost centers that provide a product or service. In turn, the associated expense is assigned to internal clients' cost centers that consume the products and services. For example, the CIO may provide all IT services within the company and assign the costs back to the business units that consume each offering.

   a. Cost allocation
   b. Bookkeeping
   c. Business mileage reimbursement rate
   d. Carbon accounting

4. . Decision-making can be regarded as the cognitive process resulting in the selection of a belief or a course of action among several alternative possibilities. Every _____ produces a final choice that may or may not prompt action.

14. Cost Allocation, Customer-Profitability Analysis, and Sales Variance A ...

89

CHAPTER QUIZ: KEY TERMS, PEOPLE, PLACES, CONCEPTS

Decision making is one of the central activities of management and is a huge part of any process of implementation.

a. Consumer Credit Protection Act

b. manufacturing cost

c. Decision-making process

d. Social Security Act

5. _____ is the process used by companies to reduce their costs and increase their profits. Depending on a company's services or Product, the strategies can vary. Every decision in the product development process affects cost.

a. Total cost

b. manufacturing cost

c. Cost reduction

d. Health Care and Education Reconciliation Act

1. b

2. c

3. a

4. c

5. c

---

15. Allocation of Support-Department Costs, Common Costs, and Revenues

CHAPTER OUTLINE: KEY TERMS, PEOPLE, PLACES, CONCEPTS

_____	Process costing
_____	Decision-making process
_____	Cost reduction
_____	Matrix method
_____	Cost-plus contract
_____	Cost accounting

CHAPTER HIGHLIGHTS & NOTES: KEY TERMS, PEOPLE, PLACES, CONCEPTS

Process costing	Process costing is a accounting methodology that traces and accumulates direct costs, and allocates indirect costs of a manufacturing process. Costs are assigned to products, usually in a large batch, which might include an entire month's production. Eventually, costs have to be allocated to individual units of product.
Decision-making process	Decision-making can be regarded as the cognitive process resulting in the selection of a belief or a course of action among several alternative possibilities. Every decision-making process produces a final choice that may or may not prompt action. Decision making is one of the central activities of management and is a huge part of any process of implementation.
Cost reduction	Cost reduction is the process used by companies to reduce their costs and increase their profits. Depending on a company's services or Product, the strategies can vary. Every decision in the product development process affects cost.
Matrix method	The matrix method is a structural analysis method used as a fundamental principle in many applications in civil engineering.

The method is carried out, using either a stiffness matrix or a flexibility matrix. 'The flexibility method is not conducive to computer programming' - Weaver, Gere. |
| Cost-plus contract | A cost-plus contract, also termed a cost reimbursement contract, is a contract where a contractor is paid for all of its allowed expenses to a set limit plus additional payment to allow for a profit. |

15. Allocation of Support-Department Costs, Common Costs, and Revenues

	Cost-reimbursement contracts contrast with fixed-price contract, in which the contractor is paid a negotiated amount regardless of incurred expenses. Cost-plus contracts first came into use in the United States during the World Wars to encourage wartime production by large American companies.
Cost accounting	Cost accounting is a complex process of collecting, analyzing, summarizing and evaluating various alternative courses of action. Its goal is to advise the management on the most appropriate course of action based on the cost efficiency and capability. Cost accounting provides the detailed cost information that management needs to control current operations and plan for the future.

1. _____ is the process used by companies to reduce their costs and increase their profits. Depending on a company's services or Product, the strategies can vary. Every decision in the product development process affects cost.

   a. Total cost
   b. manufacturing cost
   c. Consumer Credit Protection Act
   d. Cost reduction

2. The _____ is a structural analysis method used as a fundamental principle in many applications in civil engineering.

   The method is carried out, using either a stiffness matrix or a flexibility matrix. 'The flexibility method is not conducive to computer programming' - Weaver, Gere.

   a. Consumer Credit Protection Act
   b. manufacturing cost
   c. Matrix method
   d. Constraints accounting

3. _____ is a accounting methodology that traces and accumulates direct costs, and allocates indirect costs of a manufacturing process. Costs are assigned to products, usually in a large batch, which might include an entire month's production. Eventually, costs have to be allocated to individual units of product.

   a. Backflush accounting
   b. Process costing
   c. Break-even
   d. Constraints accounting

4. A _____, also termed a cost reimbursement contract, is a contract where a contractor is paid for all of its allowed expenses to a set limit plus additional payment to allow for a profit. Cost-reimbursement contracts contrast with fixed-price contract, in which the contractor is paid a negotiated amount regardless of incurred expenses. _____s first came into use in the United States during the World Wars to encourage wartime production by large American companies.

a. Consumer Credit Protection Act
b. manufacturing cost
c. Health Care and Education Reconciliation Act
d. Cost-plus contract

5. Decision-making can be regarded as the cognitive process resulting in the selection of a belief or a course of action among several alternative possibilities. Every _____ produces a final choice that may or may not prompt action. Decision making is one of the central activities of management and is a huge part of any process of implementation.

a. Consumer Credit Protection Act
b. Breakage
c. Break-even
d. Decision-making process

1. d
2. c
3. b
4. d
5. d

You can take the complete Chapter Practice Test

for 15. Allocation of Support-Department Costs, Common Costs, and Revenues
on all key terms, persons, places, and concepts.

Online 99 Cents

http://www.JustTheFacts101.com

Use www.JustTheFacts101.com for all your study needs

including Facts101's online interactive problem solving labs in

chemistry, statistics, mathematics, and more.

16. Cost Allocation: Joint Products and Byproducts

	CVP analysis
	Relevant cost
	Process costing

CVP analysis	Cost-volume-profit, in managerial economics, is a form of cost accounting. It is a simplified model, useful for elementary instruction and for short-run decisions.
	CVP analysis expands the use of information provided by breakeven analysis.
Relevant cost	A relevant cost is a cost that differs between alternatives being considered. It is often important for businesses to distinguish between relevant and irrelevant costs when analyzing alternatives because erroneously considering irrelevant costs can lead to unsound business decisions. Also, ignoring irrelevant data in analysis can save time and effort.
Process costing	Process costing is a accounting methodology that traces and accumulates direct costs, and allocates indirect costs of a manufacturing process. Costs are assigned to products, usually in a large batch, which might include an entire month's production. Eventually, costs have to be allocated to individual units of product.

16. Cost Allocation: Joint Products and Byproducts

1. Cost-volume-profit, in managerial economics, is a form of cost accounting. It is a simplified model, useful for elementary instruction and for short-run decisions.

   _____ expands the use of information provided by breakeven analysis.

   a. Consumer Credit Protection Act
   b. Health Care and Education Reconciliation Act
   c. CVP analysis
   d. Bachelor tax

2. _____ is a accounting methodology that traces and accumulates direct costs, and allocates indirect costs of a manufacturing process. Costs are assigned to products, usually in a large batch, which might include an entire month's production. Eventually, costs have to be allocated to individual units of product.

   a. Backflush accounting
   b. Process costing
   c. Break-even
   d. Constraints accounting

3. A _____ is a cost that differs between alternatives being considered. It is often important for businesses to distinguish between relevant and ir_____s when analyzing alternatives because erroneously considering ir_____s can lead to unsound business decisions. Also, ignoring irrelevant data in analysis can save time and effort.

   a. Backflush accounting
   b. Breakage
   c. Relevant cost
   d. Constraints accounting

1. c
2. b
3. c

You can take the complete Chapter Practice Test

for 16. Cost Allocation: Joint Products and Byproducts
on all key terms, persons, places, and concepts.

Online 99 Cents

http://www.JustTheFacts101.com

Use www.JustTheFacts101.com for all your study needs

including Facts101's online interactive problem solving labs in

chemistry, statistics, mathematics, and more.

17. Process Costing

_____	Process costing
_____	CVP analysis
_____	Journal entry
_____	Vendor-managed inventory
_____	Finished good
_____	Activity-based costing

Process costing	Process costing is a accounting methodology that traces and accumulates direct costs, and allocates indirect costs of a manufacturing process. Costs are assigned to products, usually in a large batch, which might include an entire month's production. Eventually, costs have to be allocated to individual units of product.
CVP analysis	Cost-volume-profit, in managerial economics, is a form of cost accounting. It is a simplified model, useful for elementary instruction and for short-run decisions. CVP analysis expands the use of information provided by breakeven analysis.
Journal entry	A journal entry, in accounting, is a logging of transactions into accounting journal items. The journal entry can consist of several recordings, each of which is either a debit or a credit. The total of the debits must equal the total of the credits or the journal entry is said to be 'unbalanced'.
Vendor-managed inventory	Vendor-managed inventory is a family of business models in which the buyer of a product (business) provides certain information to a vendor (supply chain) supplier of that product and the supplier takes full responsibility for maintaining an agreed inventory of the material, usually at the buyer's consumption location (usually a store). A third-party logistics provider can also be involved to make sure that the buyer has the required level of inventory by adjusting the demand and supply gaps.

Finished good	Finished goods are goods that have completed the manufacturing process but have not yet been sold or distributed to the end user.
Activity-based costing	Activity-based costing is a costing methodology that identifies activities in an organization and assigns the cost of each activity with resources to all products and services according to the actual consumption by each. This model assigns more indirect costs (overhead) into direct costs compared to conventional costing. CIMA (Chartered Institute of Management Accountants) defines Activity based costing as an approach to the costing and monitoring of activities which involves tracing resource consumption and costing final outputs.

CHAPTER QUIZ: KEY TERMS, PEOPLE, PLACES, CONCEPTS

1. _____ is a accounting methodology that traces and accumulates direct costs, and allocates indirect costs of a manufacturing process. Costs are assigned to products, usually in a large batch, which might include an entire month's production. Eventually, costs have to be allocated to individual units of product.

   a. Backflush accounting
   b. Breakage
   c. Break-even
   d. Process costing

2. Cost-volume-profit, in managerial economics, is a form of cost accounting. It is a simplified model, useful for elementary instruction and for short-run decisions.

   _____ expands the use of information provided by breakeven analysis.

   a. CVP analysis
   b. Breakage
   c. Break-even
   d. Constraints accounting

3. . A _____, in accounting, is a logging of transactions into accounting journal items. The _____ can consist of several recordings, each of which is either a debit or a credit. The total of the debits must equal the total of the credits or the _____ is said to be 'unbalanced'.

   a. Journal entry

b. Check register

c. General journal

d. General ledger

4. _____ is a costing methodology that identifies activities in an organization and assigns the cost of each activity with resources to all products and services according to the actual consumption by each. This model assigns more indirect costs (overhead) into direct costs compared to conventional costing.

CIMA (Chartered Institute of Management Accountants) defines Activity based costing as an approach to the costing and monitoring of activities which involves tracing resource consumption and costing final outputs.

a. Managerial risk accounting

b. Variable Costing

c. Activity-based costing

d. BDO International

5. _____ is a family of business models in which the buyer of a product (business) provides certain information to a vendor (supply chain) supplier of that product and the supplier takes full responsibility for maintaining an agreed inventory of the material, usually at the buyer's consumption location (usually a store). A third-party logistics provider can also be involved to make sure that the buyer has the required level of inventory by adjusting the demand and supply gaps.

As a symbiotic relationship, Vendor managed inventory makes it less likely that a business will unintentionally become out of stock of a good and reduces inventory in the supply chain.

a. Vendor-managed inventory

b. Consumer Credit Protection Act

c. Health Care and Education Reconciliation Act

d. General ledger

1. d
2. a
3. a
4. c
5. a

18. Spoilage, Rework, and Scrap

	Insourcing
	Process costing
	Finished good
	Journal entry
	Job costing

CHAPTER HIGHLIGHTS & NOTES: KEY TERMS, PEOPLE, PLACES, CONCEPTS

Insourcing	Insourcing is the cessation by a company of contracting a business function and the commencement of performing it internally. Insourcing is the opposite of outsourcing. Insourcing is a business decision that is often made to maintain control of critical production or competencies.
Process costing	Process costing is a accounting methodology that traces and accumulates direct costs, and allocates indirect costs of a manufacturing process. Costs are assigned to products, usually in a large batch, which might include an entire month's production. Eventually, costs have to be allocated to individual units of product.
Finished good	Finished goods are goods that have completed the manufacturing process but have not yet been sold or distributed to the end user.
Journal entry	A journal entry, in accounting, is a logging of transactions into accounting journal items. The journal entry can consist of several recordings, each of which is either a debit or a credit. The total of the debits must equal the total of the credits or the journal entry is said to be 'unbalanced'.
Job costing	Job Costing involves the calculation of costs involved in a construction 'job' or the manufacturing of goods done in discrete batches. These costs are recorded in ledger accounts throughout the life of the job or batch and are then summarized in the final trial balance before the preparing of the job cost or batch manufacturing statement.

18. Spoilage, Rework, and Scrap

1. A _____, in accounting, is a logging of transactions into accounting journal items. The _____ can consist of several recordings, each of which is either a debit or a credit. The total of the debits must equal the total of the credits or the _____ is said to be 'unbalanced'.

   a. Cash receipts journal
   b. Journal entry
   c. General journal
   d. General ledger

2. _____ is the cessation by a company of contracting a business function and the commencement of performing it internally. _____ is the opposite of outsourcing. _____ is a business decision that is often made to maintain control of critical production or competencies.

   a. Inter Revisjon
   b. Insourcing
   c. Accredited Business Accountant
   d. Indian Chartered Accountancy Course

3. _____ is a accounting methodology that traces and accumulates direct costs, and allocates indirect costs of a manufacturing process. Costs are assigned to products, usually in a large batch, which might include an entire month's production. Eventually, costs have to be allocated to individual units of product.

   a. Process costing
   b. Breakage
   c. Break-even
   d. Constraints accounting

4. _____s are goods that have completed the manufacturing process but have not yet been sold or distributed to the end user.

   a. Finished good
   b. Cost of goods available for sale
   c. Cost of goods sold
   d. Decomposition

5. _____ involves the calculation of costs involved in a construction 'job' or the manufacturing of goods done in discrete batches. These costs are recorded in ledger accounts throughout the life of the job or batch and are then summarized in the final trial balance before the preparing of the job cost or batch manufacturing statement.

   a. Backflush accounting
   b. Job costing
   c. Break-even
   d. Constraints accounting

1. b
2. b
3. a
4. a
5. b

19. Balanced Scorecard: Quality and Time

CHAPTER OUTLINE: KEY TERMS, PEOPLE, PLACES, CONCEPTS

	Cost reduction
	Quality costs
	Control charts
	Statistical process control
	Customer satisfaction
	Quality control
	Six Sigma
	Balanced Scorecard
	Book value
	On-time performance
	Decision-making process

CHAPTER HIGHLIGHTS & NOTES: KEY TERMS, PEOPLE, PLACES, CONCEPTS

Cost reduction	Cost reduction is the process used by companies to reduce their costs and increase their profits. Depending on a company's services or Product, the strategies can vary. Every decision in the product development process affects cost.
Quality costs	In process improvement efforts, quality costs or cost of quality is a means to quantify the total cost of quality-related efforts and deficiencies. It was first described by Armand V. Feigenbaum in a 1956 Harvard Business Review article. Prior to its introduction, the general perception was that higher quality requires higher costs, either by buying better materials or machines or by hiring more labor.

19. Balanced Scorecard: Quality and Time

Control charts	Control charts, also known as Shewhart charts or process-behavior charts, in statistical process control are tools used to determine if a manufacturing or business process is in a state of statistical control.
Statistical process control	Statistical process control is a method of quality control which uses statistical methods. Statistical process control is applied in order to monitor and control a process. Monitoring and controlling the process ensures that it operates at its full potential.
Customer satisfaction	Customer satisfaction is a term frequently used in marketing. It is a measure of how products and services supplied by a company meet or surpass customer expectation. Customer satisfaction is defined as 'the number of customers, or percentage of total customers, whose reported experience with a firm, its products, or its services (ratings) exceeds specified satisfaction goals.' In a survey of nearly 200 senior marketing managers, 71 percent responded that they found a customer satisfaction metric very useful in managing and monitoring their businesses.
Quality control	Quality control, or QC for short, is a process by which entities review the quality of all factors involved in production. This approach places an emphasis on three aspects:•Elements such as controls, job management, defined and well managed processes, performance and integrity criteria, and identification of records•Competence, such as knowledge, skills, experience, and qualifications•Soft elements, such as personnel, integrity, confidence, organizational culture, motivation, team spirit, and quality relationships. Controls include product inspection, where every product is examined visually, and often using a stereo microscope for fine detail before the product is sold into the external market. Inspectors will be provided with lists and descriptions of unacceptable product defects such as cracks or surface blemishes for example.
Six Sigma	Six Sigma is a set of techniques and tools for process improvement. It was developed by Motorola in 1986, coinciding with the Japanese asset price bubble which is reflected in its terminology. Jack Welch made it central to his business strategy at General Electric in 1995. Today, it is used in many industrial sectors.
Balanced Scorecard	The balanced scorecard is a strategy performance management tool - a semi-standard structured report, supported by design methods and automation tools, that can be used by managers to keep track of the execution of activities by the staff within their control and to monitor the consequences arising from these actions. It is perhaps the best known of several such frameworks (it was the most widely adopted performance management framework reported in the 2010 annual survey of management tools undertaken by Bain & Company)..
Book value	In accounting, book value or carrying value is the value of an asset according to its balance sheet account balance. For assets, the value is based on the original cost of the asset less any depreciation, amortization or impairment costs made against the asset.

19. Balanced Scorecard: Quality and Time

On-time performance	In transportation, such as municipal public transportation, schedule adherence or on-time performance refers to the level of success of the service remaining on the published schedule.
Decision-making process	Decision-making can be regarded as the cognitive process resulting in the selection of a belief or a course of action among several alternative possibilities. Every decision-making process produces a final choice that may or may not prompt action. Decision making is one of the central activities of management and is a huge part of any process of implementation.

1. In transportation, such as municipal public transportation, schedule adherence or _____ refers to the level of success of the service remaining on the published schedule.

   a. On-time performance
   b. Certified Public Accountant
   c. Certified Practising Accountant
   d. Certified Payroll Professional

2. _____, also known as Shewhart charts or process-behavior charts, in statistical process control are tools used to determine if a manufacturing or business process is in a state of statistical control.

   a. Consumer Credit Protection Act
   b. manufacturing cost
   c. Health Care and Education Reconciliation Act
   d. Control charts

3. _____ is a method of quality control which uses statistical methods. _____ is applied in order to monitor and control a process. Monitoring and controlling the process ensures that it operates at its full potential.

   a. Statistical process control
   b. manufacturing cost
   c. Health Care and Education Reconciliation Act
   d. Social Security Act

4. . _____ is the process used by companies to reduce their costs and increase their profits. Depending on a company's services or Product, the strategies can vary. Every decision in the product development process affects cost.

   a. Total cost
   b. manufacturing cost

c. Consumer Credit Protection Act

d. Cost reduction

5. In process improvement efforts, _____ or cost of quality is a means to quantify the total cost of quality-related efforts and deficiencies. It was first described by Armand V. Feigenbaum in a 1956 Harvard Business Review article.

Prior to its introduction, the general perception was that higher quality requires higher costs, either by buying better materials or machines or by hiring more labor.

a. Consumer Credit Protection Act

b. Quality costs

c. Health Care and Education Reconciliation Act

d. Social Security Act

1. a

2. d

3. a

4. d

5. b

You can take the complete Chapter Practice Test

for 19. Balanced Scorecard: Quality and Time
on all key terms, persons, places, and concepts.

Online 99 Cents

http://www.JustTheFacts101.com

Use www.JustTheFacts101.com for all your study needs

including Facts101's online interactive problem solving labs in

chemistry, statistics, mathematics, and more.

20. Inventory Management, Just-in-Time, and Simplified Costing Methods

CHAPTER OUTLINE: KEY TERMS, PEOPLE, PLACES, CONCEPTS

	Cost reduction
	Responsibility center
	Stockout
	Job costing
	Reorder point
	Safety stock
	Relevant cost
	Supplier evaluation
	Supply chain
	Vendor-managed inventory
	Enterprise resource planning
	Lean accounting

CHAPTER HIGHLIGHTS & NOTES: KEY TERMS, PEOPLE, PLACES, CONCEPTS

Cost reduction	Cost reduction is the process used by companies to reduce their costs and increase their profits. Depending on a company's services or Product, the strategies can vary. Every decision in the product development process affects cost.
Responsibility center	A responsibility center is an organization unit that is headed by a manager who is responsible for its activities and results. In Responsibility Accounting revenues and costs information are collected and reported by responsibility centers.
Stockout	A stockout, or out-of-stock event is an event that causes inventory to be exhausted. While out-of-stocks can occur along the entire supply chain, the most visible kind are retail out-of-stocks in the fast moving consumer goods industry (e.g., sweets, diapers, fruits).

20. Inventory Management, Just-in-Time, and Simplified Costing Methods

Job costing	Job Costing involves the calculation of costs involved in a construction 'job' or the manufacturing of goods done in discrete batches. These costs are recorded in ledger accounts throughout the life of the job or batch and are then summarized in the final trial balance before the preparing of the job cost or batch manufacturing statement.
Reorder point	The reorder point is the level of inventory when an order should be made with suppliers to bring the inventory up by the Economic order quantity ('EOQ').
Safety stock	Safety stock is a term used by logisticians to describe a level of extra stock that is maintained to mitigate risk of stockouts (shortfall in raw material or packaging) due to uncertainties in supply and demand. Adequate safety stock levels permit business operations to proceed according to their plans. Safety stock is held when there is uncertainty in the demand level or lead time for the product; it serves as an insurance against stockouts.
Relevant cost	A relevant cost is a cost that differs between alternatives being considered. It is often important for businesses to distinguish between relevant and irrelevant costs when analyzing alternatives because erroneously considering irrelevant costs can lead to unsound business decisions. Also, ignoring irrelevant data in analysis can save time and effort.
Supplier evaluation	Supplier evaluation is a term used in business and refers to the process of evaluating and approving potential suppliers by quantitative assessment. The purpose of supplier evaluation is to ensure a portfolio of best in class suppliers is available for use. Supplier evaluation is also a process applied to current suppliers in order to measure and monitor their performance for the purposes of reducing costs, mitigating risk and driving continuous improvement.
Supply chain	A supply chain is a system of organizations, people, activities, information, and resources involved in moving a product or service from supplier to customer. Supply chain activities transform natural resources, raw materials, and components into a finished product that is delivered to the end customer. In sophisticated supply chain systems, used products may re-enter the supply chain at any point where residual value is recyclable.
Vendor-managed inventory	Vendor-managed inventory is a family of business models in which the buyer of a product (business) provides certain information to a vendor (supply chain) supplier of that product and the supplier takes full responsibility for maintaining an agreed inventory of the material, usually at the buyer's consumption location (usually a store). A third-party logistics provider can also be involved to make sure that the buyer has the required level of inventory by adjusting the demand and supply gaps.
	As a symbiotic relationship, Vendor managed inventory makes it less likely that a business will unintentionally become out of stock of a good and reduces inventory in the supply chain.

Enterprise resource planning	Enterprise resource planning is a business management software--usually a suite of integrated applications--that a company can use to store and manage data from every stage of business, including: Enterprise resource planning provides an integrated real-time view of core business processes, using common databases maintained by a database management system. Enterprise resource planning systems track business resources--cash, raw materials, production capacity--and the status of business commitments: orders, purchase orders, and payroll. The applications that make up the system share data across the various departments (manufacturing, purchasing, sales, accounting, etc).
Lean accounting	The purpose of Lean Accounting is to support the lean enterprise as a business strategy. It seeks to move from traditional accounting methods to a system that measures and motivates excellent business practices in the lean enterprise.

CHAPTER QUIZ: KEY TERMS, PEOPLE, PLACES, CONCEPTS

1. A _____ is a system of organizations, people, activities, information, and resources involved in moving a product or service from supplier to customer. _____ activities transform natural resources, raw materials, and components into a finished product that is delivered to the end customer. In sophisticated _____ systems, used products may re-enter the _____ at any point where residual value is recyclable.

   a. Vendor-managed inventory
   b. Stockout
   c. Consumer Credit Protection Act
   d. Supply chain

2. _____ is a business management software--usually a suite of integrated applications--that a company can use to store and manage data from every stage of business, including:

   _____ provides an integrated real-time view of core business processes, using common databases maintained by a database management system. _____ systems track business resources--cash, raw materials, production capacity--and the status of business commitments: orders, purchase orders, and payroll. The applications that make up the system share data across the various departments (manufacturing, purchasing, sales, accounting, etc).

   a. Inter Revisjon
   b. Accountant
   c. Accredited Business Accountant
   d. Enterprise resource planning

3. _____ is a term used by logisticians to describe a level of extra stock that is maintained to mitigate risk of stockouts (shortfall in raw material or packaging) due to uncertainties in supply and demand. Adequate _____ levels permit business operations to proceed according to their plans. _____ is held when there is uncertainty in the demand level or lead time for the product; it serves as an insurance against stockouts.

   a. Safety stock
   b. Cost of goods available for sale
   c. Cost of goods sold
   d. Decomposition

4. The _____ is the level of inventory when an order should be made with suppliers to bring the inventory up by the Economic order quantity ('EOQ').

   a. Carrying cost
   b. Reorder point
   c. Cost of goods sold
   d. Decomposition

5. _____ is the process used by companies to reduce their costs and increase their profits. Depending on a company's services or Product, the strategies can vary. Every decision in the product development process affects cost.

   a. Cost reduction
   b. manufacturing cost
   c. Consumer Credit Protection Act
   d. Health Care and Education Reconciliation Act

1. d

2. d

3. a

4. b

5. a

You can take the complete Chapter Practice Test

for 20. Inventory Management, Just-in-Time, and Simplified Costing Methods
on all key terms, persons, places, and concepts.

Online 99 Cents

http://www.JustTheFacts101.com

Use www.JustTheFacts101.com for all your study needs

including Facts101's online interactive problem solving labs in

chemistry, statistics, mathematics, and more.

CHAPTER OUTLINE: KEY TERMS, PEOPLE, PLACES, CONCEPTS

Capital budgeting

Decision-making process

Cost reduction

Opportunity cost

Opportunity cost of capital

Time value of money

Cash flow

Present value

Discounted cash flow

Sensitivity analysis

Working capital

Project management

Industrial engineering

21. Capital Budgeting and Cost Analysis

Capital budgeting	Capital budgeting is the planning process used to determine whether an organization's long term investments such as new machinery, replacement machinery, new plants, new products, and research development projects are worth the funding of cash through the firm's capitalization structure (debt, equity or retained earnings). It is the process of allocating resources for major capital, or investment, expenditures. One of the primary goals of capital budgeting investments is to increase the value of the firm to the shareholders.
Decision-making process	Decision-making can be regarded as the cognitive process resulting in the selection of a belief or a course of action among several alternative possibilities. Every decision-making process produces a final choice that may or may not prompt action. Decision making is one of the central activities of management and is a huge part of any process of implementation.
Cost reduction	Cost reduction is the process used by companies to reduce their costs and increase their profits. Depending on a company's services or Product, the strategies can vary. Every decision in the product development process affects cost.
Opportunity cost	In microeconomic theory, the opportunity cost of a choice is the value of the best alternative forgone, in a situation in which a choice needs to be made between several mutually exclusive alternatives given limited resources. Assuming the best choice is made, it is the 'cost' incurred by not enjoying the benefit that would be had by taking the second best choice available. The New Oxford American Dictionary defines it as 'the loss of potential gain from other alternatives when one alternative is chosen'.
Opportunity cost of capital	The opportunity cost of capital is the expected rate of return forgone by bypassing of other potential investment activities for a given capital. It is a rate of return that investors could earn in financial markets.
Time value of money	The time value of money is the principle that the purchasing power of money can vary over time; money today might have a different purchasing power than money a decade later. The value of money at a future point in time might be calculated by accounting for interest earned or inflation accrued. The time value of money is the central concept in finance theory.
Cash flow	Cash flow is the movement of money into or out of a business, project, or financial product. It is usually measured during a specified, limited period of time. Measurement of cash flow can be used for calculating other parameters that give information on a company's value and situation.
Present value	Present value, also known as present discounted value, is a future amount of money that has been discounted to reflect its current value, as if it existed today. The present value is always less than or equal to the future value because money has interest-earning potential, a characteristic referred to as the time value of money. Time value can be described with the simplified phrase, "A dollar today is worth more than a dollar tomorrow".

21. Capital Budgeting and Cost Analysis

123

CHAPTER HIGHLIGHTS & NOTES: KEY TERMS, PEOPLE, PLACES, CONCEPTS

Discounted cash flow	In finance, discounted cash flow analysis is a method of valuing a project, company, or asset using the concepts of the time value of money. All future cash flows are estimated and discounted to give their present values (PVs)--the sum of all future cash flows, both incoming and outgoing, is the net present value (NPV), which is taken as the value or price of the cash flows in question. Present value may also be expressed as a number of years' purchase of the future undiscounted annual cash flows expected to arise.
Sensitivity analysis	Sensitivity analysis is the study of how the uncertainty in the output of a mathematical model or system can be apportioned to different sources of uncertainty in its inputs. A related practice is uncertainty analysis, which has a greater focus on uncertainty quantification and propagation of uncertainty. Ideally, uncertainty and sensitivity analysis should be run in tandem.
Working capital	Working capital is a financial metric which represents operating liquidity available to a business, organization or other entity, including governmental entity. Along with fixed assets such as plant and equipment, working capital is considered a part of operating capital. Gross working capital equals to current assets.
Project management	Project management is the process and activity of planning, organizing, motivating, and controlling resources, procedures and protocols to achieve specific goals in scientific or daily problems. A project is a temporary endeavor designed to produce a unique product, service or result with a defined beginning and end (usually time-constrained, and often constrained by funding or deliverables), undertaken to meet unique goals and objectives, typically to bring about beneficial change or added value. The temporary nature of projects stands in contrast with business as usual (or operations), which are repetitive, permanent, or semi-permanent functional activities to produce products or services.
Industrial engineering	Industrial engineering is a branch of engineering dealing with the optimization of complex processes or systems. It is concerned with the development, improvement, implementation and evaluation of integrated systems of people, money, knowledge, information, equipment, energy, materials, analysis and synthesis, as well as the mathematical, physical and social sciences together with the principles and methods of engineering design to specify, predict, and evaluate the results to be obtained from such systems or processes. Its underlying concepts overlap considerably with certain business-oriented disciplines such as operations management.

21. Capital Budgeting and Cost Analysis

1. In finance, _____ analysis is a method of valuing a project, company, or asset using the concepts of the time value of money. All future cash flows are estimated and discounted to give their present values (PVs)--the sum of all future cash flows, both incoming and outgoing, is the net present value (NPV), which is taken as the value or price of the cash flows in question. Present value may also be expressed as a number of years' purchase of the future undiscounted annual cash flows expected to arise.

   a. Discounted cash flow
   b. Cash flow hedge
   c. Cash flow loan
   d. Bachelor tax

2. The _____ is the principle that the purchasing power of money can vary over time; money today might have a different purchasing power than money a decade later. The value of money at a future point in time might be calculated by accounting for interest earned or inflation accrued. The _____ is the central concept in finance theory.

   a. Bill of credit
   b. Billionaire
   c. Cash
   d. Time value of money

3. _____ is the planning process used to determine whether an organization's long term investments such as new machinery, replacement machinery, new plants, new products, and research development projects are worth the funding of cash through the firm's capitalization structure (debt, equity or retained earnings). It is the process of allocating resources for major capital, or investment, expenditures. One of the primary goals of _____ investments is to increase the value of the firm to the shareholders.

   a. Consumer Credit Protection Act
   b. Health Care and Education Reconciliation Act
   c. Social Security Act
   d. Capital budgeting

4. _____ is the process used by companies to reduce their costs and increase their profits. Depending on a company's services or Product, the strategies can vary. Every decision in the product development process affects cost.

   a. Total cost
   b. manufacturing cost
   c. Consumer Credit Protection Act
   d. Cost reduction

5. . _____ is a branch of engineering dealing with the optimization of complex processes or systems.

It is concerned with the development, improvement, implementation and evaluation of integrated systems of people, money, knowledge, information, equipment, energy, materials, analysis and synthesis, as well as the mathematical, physical and social sciences together with the principles and methods of engineering design to specify, predict, and evaluate the results to be obtained from such systems or processes. Its underlying concepts overlap considerably with certain business-oriented disciplines such as operations management.

a. Industrial engineering
b. Staff management
c. Accountant
d. Convenience translation

1. a

2. d

3. d

4. d

5. a

CHAPTER OUTLINE: KEY TERMS, PEOPLE, PLACES, CONCEPTS

	Transfer pricing
	Management control
	Management control system
	Intermediate product
	Investment center
	Profit center
	Revenue center
	Responsibility center
	Perfectly competitive
	Imperfect competition

CHAPTER HIGHLIGHTS & NOTES: KEY TERMS, PEOPLE, PLACES, CONCEPTS

Transfer pricing	Transfer pricing is a profit allocation method used to attribute a multinational corporation's net profit (or loss) before tax to countries where it does business.
	Transfer pricing results in the setting of prices among divisions within an enterprise. Transfer prices are charges for goods and services between controlled (or related) legal entities, i.e., within an enterprise.
Management control	A management control system is a system which gathers and uses information to evaluate the performance of different organizational resources like human, physical, financial and also the organization as a whole considering the organizational strategies. Finally, MCS influences the behavior of organizational resources to implement organizational strategies. MCS might be formal or informal.

22. Management Control Systems, Transfer Pricing, and Multinational Consid ...

Management control system	A management control system is a system which gathers and uses information to evaluate the performance of different organizational resources like human, physical, financial and also the organization as a whole considering the organizational strategies. Finally, Management control system influences the behavior of organizational resources to implement organizational strategies. Management control system might be formal or informal.
Intermediate product	An intermediate product is a product that might require further processing before it is saleable to the ultimate consumer. This further processing might be done by the producer or by another processor. Thus, an intermediate product might be a final product for one company and an input for another company that will process it further.
Investment center	An investment center is a classification used for business units within an enterprise. The essential element of an investment center is that it is treated as a unit which is measured against its use of capital, as opposed to a cost or profit center, which are measured against raw costs or profits. The Investment Center takes care of Revenues, Cost and Assets -while Profit Center deal just with revenues and costs and Cost Center with cost only.
Profit center	A profit center is a part of a corporation that directly adds to its profit.
Revenue center	In business, a revenue centre or revenue center is a division that gains revenue from product sales or service provided. The manager in revenue centre is accountable for revenue only.
Responsibility center	A responsibility center is an organization unit that is headed by a manager who is responsible for its activities and results. In Responsibility Accounting revenues and costs information are collected and reported by responsibility centers.
Perfectly competitive	In economic theory, perfect competition describes markets such that no participants are large enough to have the market power to set the price of a homogeneous product. Because the conditions for perfect competition are strict, there are few if any perfectly competitive markets. Still, buyers and sellers in some auction-type markets, say for commodities or some financial assets, may approximate the concept.
Imperfect competition	In economic theory, imperfect competition is a type of market structure showing some but not all features of competitive markets. Forms of imperfect competition include:•Oligopoly, in which there are few sellers of a product.•Monopolistic competition, in which there are many sellers producing highly differentiated products.•Monopsony, where there are many sellers but only one buyer, and oligopsony, where there are many sellers but few buyers..

1. _____ is a profit allocation method used to attribute a multinational corporation's net profit (or loss) before tax to countries where it does business.

   _____ results in the setting of prices among divisions within an enterprise. Transfer prices are charges for goods and services between controlled (or related) legal entities, i.e., within an enterprise.

   a. Bank tax
   b. Transfer pricing
   c. Cross-border leasing
   d. Currency transaction tax

2. A _____ system is a system which gathers and uses information to evaluate the performance of different organizational resources like human, physical, financial and also the organization as a whole considering the organizational strategies. Finally, MCS influences the behavior of organizational resources to implement organizational strategies. MCS might be formal or informal.

   a. Management control
   b. Controlled foreign corporation
   c. Cross-border leasing
   d. Currency transaction tax

3. In business, a revenue centre or _____ is a division that gains revenue from product sales or service provided. The manager in revenue centre is accountable for revenue only.

   a. Balance
   b. Capital appreciation
   c. Capital expenditure
   d. Revenue center

4. A _____ is a part of a corporation that directly adds to its profit.

   a. Backflush accounting
   b. Breakage
   c. Profit center
   d. Constraints accounting

5. . An _____ is a classification used for business units within an enterprise. The essential element of an _____ is that it is treated as a unit which is measured against its use of capital, as opposed to a cost or profit center, which are measured against raw costs or profits.

   The _____ takes care of Revenues, Cost and Assets -while Profit Center deal just with revenues and costs and Cost Center with cost only.

   a. Backflush accounting

b. Breakage

c. Break-even

d. Investment center

1. b
2. a
3. d
4. c
5. d

You can take the complete Chapter Practice Test

for 22. Management Control Systems, Transfer Pricing, and Multinational Consid ...
on all key terms, persons, places, and concepts.

Online 99 Cents

http://www.JustTheFacts101.com

Use www.JustTheFacts101.com for all your study needs

including Facts101's online interactive problem solving labs in

chemistry, statistics, mathematics, and more.

CHAPTER OUTLINE: KEY TERMS, PEOPLE, PLACES, CONCEPTS

	Balanced Scorecard
	Management control
	Accounting rate of return
	Responsibility center
	Return on Investment
	Job costing
	Economic value
	Economic Value Added
	Time horizon
	Asset
	Equity
	Moral hazard
	Belief systems
	Error term

23. Performance Measurement, Compensation, and Multinational Consideration ...

Balanced Scorecard	The balanced scorecard is a strategy performance management tool - a semi-standard structured report, supported by design methods and automation tools, that can be used by managers to keep track of the execution of activities by the staff within their control and to monitor the consequences arising from these actions. It is perhaps the best known of several such frameworks (it was the most widely adopted performance management framework reported in the 2010 annual survey of management tools undertaken by Bain & Company)..
Management control	A management control system is a system which gathers and uses information to evaluate the performance of different organizational resources like human, physical, financial and also the organization as a whole considering the organizational strategies. Finally, MCS influences the behavior of organizational resources to implement organizational strategies. MCS might be formal or informal.
Accounting rate of return	Accounting rate of return, also known as the Average rate of return, or ARR is a financial ratio used in capital budgeting. The ratio does not take into account the concept of time value of money. ARR calculates the return, generated from net income of the proposed capital investment.
Responsibility center	A responsibility center is an organization unit that is headed by a manager who is responsible for its activities and results. In Responsibility Accounting revenues and costs information are collected and reported by responsibility centers.
Return on Investment	Return on investment is the concept of an investment of some resource yielding a benefit to the investor. A high return on Investment means the investment gains compare favorably to investment cost. As a performance measure, return on Investment is used to evaluate the efficiency of an investment or to compare the efficiency of a number of different investments.
Job costing	Job Costing involves the calculation of costs involved in a construction 'job' or the manufacturing of goods done in discrete batches. These costs are recorded in ledger accounts throughout the life of the job or batch and are then summarized in the final trial balance before the preparing of the job cost or batch manufacturing statement.
Economic value	Economic value is a measure of the benefit that an economic actor can gain from either a good or service. It is generally measured relative to units of currency, and the interpretation is therefore 'what is the maximum amount of money a specific actor is willing and able to pay for the good or service'?
	Note that economic value is not the same as market price. If a consumer is willing to buy a good, it implies that the customer places a higher value on the good than the market price.
Economic Value Added	In corporate finance, Economic Value Added, is an estimate of a firm's economic profit - being the value created in excess of the required return of the company's investors (being shareholders and debt holders).

	Quite simply, Economic Value Added® is the profit earned by the firm less the cost of financing the firm's capital. The idea is that value is created when the return on the firm's economic capital employed is greater than the cost of that capital.
Time horizon	A time horizon, also known as a planning horizon, is a fixed point of time in the future at which point certain processes will be evaluated or assumed to end. It is necessary in an accounting, finance or risk management regime to assign such a fixed horizon time so that alternatives can be evaluated for performance over the same period of time. A time horizon is a physical impossibility in the real world.
Asset	In financial accounting, an asset is an economic resource. Anything tangible or intangible that is capable of being owned or controlled to produce value and that is held to have positive economic value is considered an asset. Simply stated, assets represent value of ownership that can be converted into cash (although cash itself is also considered an asset).
Equity	In accounting and finance, equity is the residual claimant or interest of the most junior class of investors in assets, after all liabilities are paid; if liability exceeds assets, negative equity exists. In an accounting context, shareholders' equity represents the remaining interest in the assets of a company, spread among individual shareholders of common or preferred stock; a negative shareholders' equity is often referred to as a positive shareholders' deficit. At the start of a business, owners put some funding into the business to finance operations.
Moral hazard	In economic theory, a moral hazard is a situation where a party will have a tendency to take risks because the costs that could result will not be felt by the party taking the risk. In other words, it is a tendency to be more willing to take a risk, knowing that the potential costs or burdens of taking such risk will be borne, in whole or in part, by others. A moral hazard may occur where the actions of one party may change to the detriment of another after a financial transaction has taken place.
Belief systems	A belief system is a set of mutually supportive beliefs. The beliefs of any such system can be classified as religious, philosophical, ideological, or a combination of these. Philosopher Jonathan Glover says that beliefs are always part of a belief system, and that belief systems are difficult to completely revise.
Error term	An error term is an additive type of error. Common examples include:•errors and residuals in statistics, e.g. in linear regression•the error term in numerical integration.

1. In corporate finance, _____, is an estimate of a firm's economic profit - being the value created in excess of the required return of the company's investors (being shareholders and debt holders). Quite simply, _____® is the profit earned by the firm less the cost of financing the firm's capital. The idea is that value is created when the return on the firm's economic capital employed is greater than the cost of that capital.

   a. Business valuation standard
   b. Economic Value Added
   c. Bachelor tax
   d. BDO International

2. The _____ is a strategy performance management tool - a semi-standard structured report, supported by design methods and automation tools, that can be used by managers to keep track of the execution of activities by the staff within their control and to monitor the consequences arising from these actions. It is perhaps the best known of several such frameworks (it was the most widely adopted performance management framework reported in the 2010 annual survey of management tools undertaken by Bain & Company)..

   a. Consumer Credit Protection Act
   b. Certified Quality Auditor
   c. Chief audit executive
   d. Balanced Scorecard

3. In accounting and finance, _____ is the residual claimant or interest of the most junior class of investors in assets, after all liabilities are paid; if liability exceeds assets, negative _____ exists. In an accounting context, shareholders' _____ represents the remaining interest in the assets of a company, spread among individual shareholders of common or preferred stock; a negative shareholders' _____ is often referred to as a positive shareholders' deficit.

   At the start of a business, owners put some funding into the business to finance operations.

   a. Book value
   b. Cash method of accounting
   c. Equity
   d. Consolidation

4. In financial accounting, an _____ is an economic resource. Anything tangible or intangible that is capable of being owned or controlled to produce value and that is held to have positive economic value is considered an _____. Simply stated, _____s represent value of ownership that can be converted into cash (although cash itself is also considered an _____).

   a. Bachelor tax
   b. BDO International
   c. Big Four
   d. Asset

5. A _____ system is a system which gathers and uses information to evaluate the performance of different organizational resources like human, physical, financial and also the organization as a whole considering the organizational strategies. Finally, MCS influences the behavior of organizational resources to implement organizational strategies. MCS might be formal or informal.

    a. Management control
    b. Certified Quality Auditor
    c. Chief audit executive
    d. Circulation Verification Council

1. b
2. d
3. c
4. d
5. a

You can take the complete Chapter Practice Test

for 23. Performance Measurement, Compensation, and Multinational Consideration ...
on all key terms, persons, places, and concepts.

Online 99 Cents

http://www.JustTheFacts101.com

Use www.JustTheFacts101.com for all your study needs

including Facts101's online interactive problem solving labs in

chemistry, statistics, mathematics, and more.

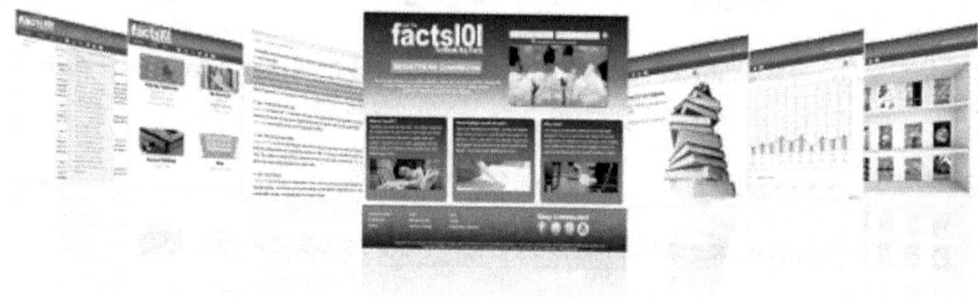

CPSIA information can be obtained
at www.ICGtesting.com
Printed in the USA
LVHW052224080721
692196LV00008B/691